COPING WITH CONFLICT

An "Elementary" Approach

By Diane S. Senn and Gwen M. Sitsch

Illustrated by Merita D. Derrick

YouthLight, Inc.

© 1996 by
YouthLight, Inc.
Chapin, SC 29036

Illustrations by Merita D. Derrick
Computer illustrations by Kimberly Grummond
Desktop Publishing by Kimberly Grummond
Reviewed by Norma Colwell, Sandie Ellis, and Kim "Tip" Frank

ISBN   1-889636-00-2
Library of Congress Catalog No. 96061189

10   9   8   7   6   5   4   3   2   1
Printed in the United States of America

For more information contact:
YouthLight, Inc. • P.O. Box 115 • Chapin, SC 29036
Phone (803) 345-1070 • (800) 209-9774 • Fax (803) 345-0888 • E-mail *YLDR1@aol.com*

DEDICATION

To my husband, Stan, for the gift of freedom to grow professionally and for the support and encouragement you have given

and to my children, Bryan and Lindsay, for the spark you ignited with your enthusiasm for this adventure.

d.s.

To Diane for inviting me on this journey

and to Mike for giving me the freedom and encouragement to go.

g.s.

SPECIAL THANKS

We extend our heartfelt thanks to the following people:

to Dr. Bob Bowman for believing in our ideas and encouraging us to embark on this venture and for being a rain shower when our ideas were running dry;

to Rita Derrick for sharing her talent and bringing *Coping with Conflict* to life with her artwork;

to Kimberly Grummond for the computer illustrations and for typing, phoning, connecting with people, and tying up all the loose ends to complete publication of this book;

to Norma Colwell, Sandie Ellis, and Kim "Tip" Frank for reviewing the manuscript and providing helpful suggestions.

to Claire Thompson for having faith in our ideas and for not only allowing us to implement the program at Chapin Elementary School but also for being our head cheerleader;

to the staff of Chapin Elementary School for giving *Coping With Conflict* wings;

to the elementary school counselors in School District Five of Lexington and Richland Counties for being colleagues extraordinaire;

to many South Carolina school counselors for the enthusiasm they showed for our program when we originally presented it at the South Carolina School Counselors and South Carolina Counselor Associations Conferences. Your confidence in the program inspired us to pursue this endeavor;

to our husbands and children--Stan, Bryan, and Lindsay Senn and Mike and Shuler Sitsch--for the sacrifices that they have tolerated in the name of *Coping With Conflict;*

and to our parents, Armand and Junell Shealy and Thomas and Kay McAlhany, for believing in us from the moment they first saw us and for their constant support and guidance.

Merely saying "thank you" seems so meager, but please know that we sincerely appreciate all that you have done to support, encourage, and inspire us.

And most importantly, we give honor and thanks to God without whom none of this would be possible.

TABLE OF CONTENTS

RATIONALE FOR CONFLICT RESOLUTION PROGRAMS

No one will dispute the fact that violence is on the rise in our nation. More and more, school-aged children are adopting violent means to express anger and work out conflicts. While there is no one cause to the rise in violence, the influences that children receive at a young age and throughout their lives play a large part in the methods they adopt to cope with conflict. There are many influences on children: family members, child care providers, peers, and television are among a few.

Conflict resolution has been getting much attention in educational literature over the past twelve years. Teaching students the skills of conflict resolution has been seen as a step to alleviating the rise in violence. Many states and school districts around the nation are adopting conflict resolution programs. Some states, such as South Carolina and Texas, have enacted legislation mandating such programs for students as well as school professionals (Carruthers, Carruthers, Day-Vines, Bostick, and Watson, 1996).

We propose three reasons for teaching elementary-aged students skills of conflict resolution: building resiliency in students, improving school climate, and the link between character education and conflict resolution.

Resiliency in children is the ability to overcome risks and avoid negative outcomes. One personal characteristic of resilient children includes an active approach to problem solving (Rak and Patterson, 1996). Rak and Patterson (1996) suggest conflict resolution techniques that assist in working through interpersonal struggles will enhance self-concept. They also purport that a proactive perspective is a factor of resilient children. Conflict resolution techniques teach students to become proactive in resolving conflict rather than becoming a scapegoat or a bully.

Oftentimes students resort to physical or verbal intimidation tactics to resolve conflicts. We've all heard, "You play what I want or I won't ever play with you again!" A child who has suffered even mild victimization may see school as an unhappy setting (Hoover and Hazler, 1991). School climate has been noted as a critical variable in student achievement. When school professionals ignore, play down, or in any way tolerate violent means of conflict resolution, they make a demeaning statement to their students regarding their worth. Students who perceive that they are safe and feel comfortable learn more. School professionals can relay a strong positive message about the worth of the individuals in their school by insuring that peaceful conflict resolution is an integral part of their school program (Hoover and Hazler, 1991).

Many school districts are now making a strong push toward character education as part of the school curriculum. Sweeney and Carruthers (1996) see character education and conflict resolution "as anchoring ends of a continuum pertaining to constructive socialized behavior." Character education and conflict resolution are related in that character education focuses on traits of the self, the intrapersonal, while conflict resolution focuses on relationships with others, the interpersonal. Together the two promote acceptable social skills.

Finally, it is to be noted that whatever conflict resolution program you choose for students needs to include an experiential aspect that allows students to practice what they learn (Sweeney and Carruthers, 1996). Teaching isolated skills without these skills being practiced or easily transferred to everyday living is teaching in vain.

Since children form behavior patterns early, often before they come to a formal leaning experience, educators are often challenged by having to "undo the damage." Conflict resolution programs, such as *Coping with Conflict: An "Elementary" Approach*, provide a structured way of teaching and practicing the skills necessary to appropriately manage conflicts.

References

Carruthers, W., Carruthers, B., Day-Vines, N., Bostick, D., & Watson, D. (1996). Conflict Resolution as Curriculum: A Definition, Description, and Process for Integration in Core Curricula. *The School Counselor*, 43, 345-373.

Hoover, J., & Hazler, R. (1991). Bullies and Victims. *Elementary School Guidance and Counseling*, 25(3), 212-219.

Rak, C., & Patterson, L. (1996). Promoting Resilience in At-Risk Children. *Journal of Counseling and Development*, 74(4), 368-373.

Sweeney, B., & Carruthers, W. (1996). Conflict Resolution: History, Philosophy, Theory, and Educational Applications. *The School Counselor*, 43, 326-344.

A NOTE TO OUR FELLOW EDUCATORS

Pick up any educational journal lately and chances are you will see an article that deals with violence in our schools. Whether it be child against child or child against teacher, violence is becoming more and more commonplace.

Experts have purported that the solution to violence is to teach conflict resolution skills to students. Anyone who has taken a look at educational material recently will quickly note that the educational market has been bombarded with programs that teach conflict resolution. One can quickly feel overwhelmed when previewing materials on this topic.

However, we have developed a conflict *management* program that we feel is simple to teach and easy for students to transfer to real–life situations. We chose the term conflict management as opposed to conflict resolution because all conflicts cannot and will not be resolved. We feel it is important to teach students that if conflicts cannot be resolved, that they can be managed in a peaceful way.

It is important to take time to teach children skills and strategies for handling conflicts. These skills are too important to be left to chance to learn. In some cases they may not be learned at all. Educators need to reach children during the elementary years as children are already forming their patterns for handling problems. If children learn the skills early, they can use these same skills throughout their lives.

Teaching is more than just sharing information one time. Teaching involves presenting that information and then reinforcing it and relating the information to real–life situations. Our program provides not only the skill information to present to students but also additional ways to reinforce these skills: the *Coping With Conflict* poster, the hands–on Timely Tools box containing twelve strategies for managing conflicts, puppet show scripts, and parent information. Our goal is for students to learn these skills so that they manage conflicts appropriately.

Thank you for choosing *Coping With Conflict: An "Elementary" Approach* and for joining us in our care and concern for children. We would enjoy hearing from you as you implement this program. Please address any comments, ideas, and/or suggestions that you may have to YouthLight, Inc. at the address given on the cover page.

Enjoy!

Diane and Gwen

INTRODUCTION

What is *Coping with Conflict* about?

Coping with Conflict: An "Elementary" Approach is a planned program designed to teach elementary aged students how to manage conflicts in a peaceful way. The program focuses on four skill areas as indicated on the accompanying *Coping With Conflict* poster: FACTS FIRST, MADNESS MANAGEMENT, CARING COMMUNICATION, and TIMELY TOOLS. The program includes classroom lessons, supplementary ideas, parent information, and follow–up puppet show scripts.

I hear and read a lot about conflict resolution. You use the term conflict management. What's the difference?

Conflict is a part of everyday living. Since all people are different, conflicts will occur. All conflicts, however, cannot be resolved. Therefore, it is important to teach students to *manage* conflicts. This means working toward a resolution but also accepting that all conflicts cannot and will not be resolved through any effort. Thus, it is important to teach students that while conflicts cannot be resolved that they can be peacefully managed.

Why is teaching conflict management so important?

Read any newspaper or listen to any news show and chances are you will read or hear of some incidence of violence. Conflicts do not produce violence. Inappropriate ways that people choose to handle conflicts can lead to violence. Children do not inherently know how to manage conflicts. Children tend to be egocentric and this complicates how they perceive conflict situations. Therefore, in order for students to learn to manage conflicts, they must be *taught* how to do this and then be allowed the opportunity to *practice* what they have learned so that appropriate conflict management becomes a part of who they are.

There are many conflict resolution programs on the market today. What makes yours unique?

Coping With Conflict: An "Elementary" Approach is unique in that it is designed for the elementary aged student. The program can easily be taught to students in grades 1–5. *Coping With Conflict* narrows the focus for conflict management to four skills: FACTS FIRST, MADNESS MANAGEMENT, CARING COMMUNICATION, and TIMELY TOOLS. Additionally, the program is simple to teach and easy for students to transfer to real–life situations. The common language that students learn in the area of conflict management is of great benefit to both students and teachers. Finally, the program includes many visuals that aid in student retention of the information. A *Coping With Conflict* poster summarizes the four skill areas of the program and the Timely Tools box provides hands–on manipulatives to facilitate the learning of twelve strategies in managing conflicts.

◆ **FACTS FIRST:** When a conflict arises, it is important to get all the facts before making any assumptions about the cause of the conflict. Many conflicts escalate because the persons involved jumped to conclusions. In order to be fair to all involved, getting the facts is the initial step in working toward a solution. Getting the facts involves asking questions to find out exactly what happened to begin the conflict. Students should be taught how to ask questions in a non–accusing manner. Many times a problem or conflict can be diverted by simply getting the facts first.

◆ **MADNESS MANAGEMENT:** Anger is a normal emotion when conflicts occur. Many times conflicts begin with a situation where anger runs high. In order to prevent a conflict from escalating, it is essential to learn to manage madness. Students should be taught three basic rules for managing madness: 1) I may not hurt myself; 2) I may not hurt someone else; and 3) I may not hurt property. A trap that everyone can fall into when they are angry is "fouling." A foul in a conflict situation can be defined as anything that is said or done that hurts someone else's feelings or body. Fouls may include: bullying, shoving, hitting, calling names, bossing, making excuses, getting revenge, teasing, or threatening.

Practically all students understand the concept of a referee and fouls. Students have either seen a sporting event or participated in sports activities themselves. The use of the referee makes this concept simple to understand. Students are to be encouraged to be their own referee, since there may be no one else to do so when they are having a conflict with another person.

It is to be emphasized that fouls make conflicts worse. Nothing can be gained by fouling. If conflicts are to be solved in a peaceful way, fouls are to be avoided.

As we have stated, anger is a normal emotion. Holding anger in produces feelings of stress and frustration. Therefore, students need to be taught constructive ways to release anger. These may include counting to ten when anger starts to take over, talking to someone uninvolved in the conflict about angry feelings, or doing something to release anger energy such as riding a bike, drawing, or listening to music.

◆ **CARING COMMUNICATION:** One of the most difficult parts of working out a conflict is knowing what to say to the other person and how to say it. Communication becomes a trap at times when conflicts occur. It is important for students to know that in order to work through conflicts they must communicate in a caring way.

Communication has two parts—the listener and the speaker. Each has a job when conflicts are being talked out. Each role should be taught.

The role of the listener in caring communication is to practice active listening skills. This includes making eye contact with the speaker, using appropriate body language that does not block communication, and saying something back that shows listening. We reemphasize that the skills must be taught. Often we assume that children know how to listen, but in actuality, not listening is a foul that occurs very often and makes conflicts escalate.

The role of the speaker is to send an "I" message. This communicates how one feels. The four steps involved in an "I" message include: say the person's name; say how you feel; tell why you feel that way; and tell what you want.

Students should be taught that since each person is different, we will have different thoughts and opinions. Therefore, something that may be done or said by one person without meaning harm could be interpreted by another as hurtful.

◆ **TIMELY TOOLS:** The last skill contains many "tools" that may help solve or manage conflict. Most jobs require more than one tool. Conflicts also require more than one skill or "tool" in order to be managed peacefully. Some conflicts are diffused by simply getting the facts or sending an "I" message. Others are not. In this case, TIMELY TOOLS may be needed.

A "tool box" is made for the classroom. The "tool box" contains 12 cards that explain ways to manage conflicts. Each card contains a visual that will help students have a clearer understanding of the way the "tool" can be used.

An explanation of each "tool" follows below. The reproducible cards and information on making your own cards are given in the CLASSROOM LESSONS section of this book.

- ✔ **Postpone:** A person may choose to put off working on the conflict especially if one or both persons is angry or tired.
- ✔ **Avoid:** There are situations and/or people who can and should be avoided.
- ✔ **Ignore:** A person may choose not to get involved or to not let something become a conflict for him/her. This can prevent a conflict from getting worse.
- ✔ **Apologize:** Say "I'm sorry" if you did something wrong. If you did nothing wrong, you may say, "I'm sorry we're having this conflict."
- ✔ **Compromise:** Sometimes both sides can give in a little and meet in the middle.
- ✔ **Chance:** Flip a coin, draw straws, or any other such luck device.
- ✔ **Humor:** Never laugh at someone, but you may laugh at a conflict if it is no big deal.
- ✔ **Share:** Find a way for all to use or enjoy together.
- ✔ **Take Turns:** Allow each to have a turn in order to be a part and enjoy.
- ✔ **Negotiate:** Problem–solve by thinking of all the possible choices and deciding on one upon which both people can agree.
- ✔ **Talk It Out:** Have a "heart to heart" where feelings are discussed in a caring way.
- ✔ **Get Help:** If a conflict is escalating, it is sometimes necessary to seek the help of an adult.

What are the essential materials required to teach this program?

The accompanying *Coping With Conflict* poster and mini–posters are essential. We recommend that each classroom have a poster and mini–posters displayed so that students are able to refer to the poster when conflicts arise. Also, each classroom will need a Timely Tools box which provides hands–on strategies for managing conflicts. The reproducible cards and information for making a Timely Tools box are given in the classroom lessons section of this book. If your school is using the program schoolwide, it is beneficial for a poster and a "tool box" to be displayed in all areas students attend. Additional materials may be needed for classroom lessons and are listed in each lesson's introduction.

What are the program components?

Classroom lessons including the *Coping With Conflict* poster and Timely Tools box comprise the main component. Parent information is provided through reproducible school newsletter articles and reproducible letters to parents as a classroom lesson follow–up. Another component is the puppet shows. These provide a creative reinforcement of the skills taught. Five scripts for these puppet shows are provided in *Coping With Conflict*.

How do all the components come together?

Basically there are four essentials. First, classroom lessons introduce the skills. Secondly, practice and reinforcement is provided through the use of the common language, role play, the *Coping With Conflict* poster, the use of the Timely Tools box, and the puppet shows. Third, there is home reinforcement using the school newsletter articles and parent letters. Finally, referring students to use the skills and the tool box when conflicts arise transfers the learning to individual conflicts. This is the most important part of the program.

Who can teach this program?

The program is designed to be taught by classroom teachers, school counselors, or school administrators. The program can be used in one classroom but is most beneficial when implemented as a schoolwide conflict management program.

What training is needed to teach the program?

No extensive training is necessary. Information needed is provided in this book. Its user–friendly format makes it simple to teach.

How much time is needed to teach the program?

We recommend one lesson per week for four weeks. However, this can be adapted to suit your needs. The program can be taught in as few as four lessons or as many as 22 lessons. However, the lessons also need reinforcement as daily conflicts occur so that the skills are transferred to everyday living. Structured reinforcement is provided through role play, puppet shows, and parent information.

How can I build support for the program?

One of the most effective ways of building support for the program is educating others about it. Talk to colleagues, administrators, and parents about what you are doing in the area of conflict management. Also, model the skills taught in your interactions with your students, your colleagues, and with parents. Encourage students to use these skills they have learned when they come to you for help with a conflict.

What do I do if I meet resistance from my colleagues?

Practice what you preach. Continue to listen to their concerns in a caring way. Invite them into your class to show how the program is working. Offer your assistance to get their program off on the right foot.

How do I use this program schoolwide?

If your school chooses to implement *Coping With Conflict: An Elementary Approach* schoolwide, share the program components and the plan for your school through a staff development session. Also, for schoolwide implementation, all areas of the school utilizing the program is helpful. The students benefit from hearing the reinforcement of conflict management skills not only in the regular classroom, but also in physical education, art, music, media, speech, resource, the office, cafeteria, etc. These areas also need a *Coping With Conflict* Poster and Timely Tools box. This provides a visual and hands-on reinforcement of the program as well as verbal reinforcement through all the staff using the common language unique to this program when helping students manage their conflict.

What are some suggestions for expanding *Coping with Conflict*?

Let your imagination run wild! Add to this program to fit the needs of your class or school. We suggest a Peace Pals Club. The Peace Pals Club members may visit in younger grades to share conflict management information and activities, plan announcements that reinforce peace skills, or create posters to display around the school that encourage the use of conflict management skills. The Peace Pals Club may also become the peer mediation team in future years.

You may also choose to have a Peace Patrol. Select a person each week from each classroom to be on the Peace Patrol. That person makes his own badge and is given a "Caught You Being Peaceful" ticket pad. His or her job for the week is to catch people in the class using appropriate conflict management skills.

Set up a conflict corner in your room. Here you may display your *Coping With Conflict* poster and your Timely Tools box. You may designate this as the area where students can go to work out conflicts. Make the area comfortable and conducive to good communication.

How do I use this book to implement a conflict management program?

◆ CLASSROOM LESSONS:

Skills can be introduced in four lessons. Check the classroom lesson section for the lessons indicated as initial lessons. Also included are supplemental classroom lessons. These supplemental lessons can be used to expand the program in the same year or may be used in subsequent years to reinforce the program.

◆ POSTER:

Display your *Coping With Conflict* poster and be ready to add the mini-posters to the outside of the main poster as the lessons are taught.

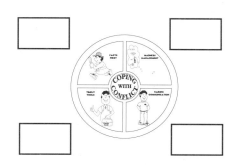

◆ TOOL BOX:

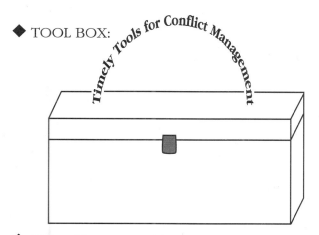

Put together your conflict management Timely Tools box. Directions and cards for reproducing this can be found on pages 55-84 in the classroom lessons section. The tool box contains a *Coping With Conflict* poster card, 12 tool cards of conflict management strategies, and role play practice cards. These need to be reproduced and placed inside a labeled Timely Tools box. The Timely Tools box will be introduced to the students as the last skill.

◆ PARENT INFORMATION:

This book contains reproducible parent letters and information to include in a school newsletter that can be shared with parents as the program is implemented. This gives parents the opportunity to not only be informed of what is being taught, but also to reinforce these conflict management skills at home with their children. Students' success in retaining these skills is increased when the skills are being taught and reinforced at school as well as home.

◆ PUPPET SHOWS:

Puppet show scripts which correlate with the conflict management skills provide a creative way to reinforce the lesson. Review the scripts and decide how you can best use these such as students from your own class putting on the show for the others, older elementary students performing the shows for the younger students, or having students act out the shows rather than using puppets.

◆ IMPORTANT COMPONENT . . . YOU!

After the lessons have been taught, find time to role play conflict situations for extra practice using the skills. Refer students to the *Coping With Conflict* poster and/or Timely Tools box when conflicts occur and use the common language unique to this program when helping students manage their conflicts. Remember--success is when the student is able to relate the learned information to real life situations.

CLASSROOM LESSONS

INTRODUCTION AND FACTS FIRST

Grade Levels:
1–5

Purpose:
Students will be able to define and recognize conflict and model getting the facts when a conflict seems to be happening.

Estimated Time:
30–35 minutes

Materials:
- *Coping With Conflict* poster
- FACTS FIRST mini–poster
- magnifying glass
- the story, *Jean is Mean* (see page 6) or *The Hating Book* by Charlotte Zolotow or *Airmail to the Moon* by Tom Birdseye

- trench coat
- (optional) a puppet
- (optional) reproducible FACTS FIRST mini-poster for each student (see page 5)

Procedures:

1. If you choose to use a puppet for your lessons on conflict management, have the puppet begin by sharing a conflict that he/she is currently having with another student in his/her class. Be sure that the conflict is applicable to teaching the FACTS FIRST component of the wheel. An example may be that the puppet said, "Good morning," to another student and that student turned and walked away without saying anything. Have the puppet become visibly upset and make assumptions about the situation.

   If you choose not to use a puppet, give an example of a conflict where it would be easy to jump to conclusions such as the one listed above.

2. Introduce the word conflict and discuss the meaning of the word. Conflict can be easily defined for students as a problem people have with each other in getting along or agreeing. Children often refer to a conflict as a fight. Be sure they understand that fighting is an inappropriate way in which people may deal with a conflict. Emphasize that conflict is a part of everyday life and that it is important to know how to manage conflicts when they arise.

3. Show the conflict poster and explain to students that they will be learning skills that will help them work out their conflicts in a peaceful way.

4. Read *Jean is Mean* or one of the stories listed above. (The stories deal with a conflict between two friends that began as a result of a misunderstanding.)

5. Discuss why the conflict occurred—someone did not know all the information before they started reacting. Point to the FACTS FIRST section on the *Coping with Conflict* poster.

6. Put on your trench coat and hold your magnifying glass. Ask students what you are. Discuss what a detective does. Ask students how being like a detective could help with a conflict.

7. Role play a student coming up behind you at the water fountain and bumping into you. Pretend

to get very angry at being bumped. Explain that you did not get the facts, but jumped to the conclusion that the person bumped into you to be mean. Replay the scene and this time encourage students to help you be a detective. Ask students to name other reasons that someone may bump into you such as someone tripping on an untied shoelace or someone behind them being pushed. Ask students how you could find out why this happened. Model asking unaccusing questions to get the facts first. Distinguish between accusing and unaccusing questions. An example of an accusing question may be, "Why are you being so mean?" An unaccusing question may be, "Is something wrong?"

8. Display the FACTS FIRST mini-poster outside the FACTS FIRST section on the *Coping With Conflict* poster and discuss appropriate questions to ask in order to get the facts.

9. Distribute copies of the reproducible FACTS FIRST mini-poster to students. (optional)

10. If you used a puppet in the set of your lesson, give the puppet a homework assignment of going back and getting the facts first.

Be certain that you emphasize to students that you have only discussed one way of handling conflict and that the others will be discussed in subsequent lessons. Ask your students to practice this skill until the next lesson.

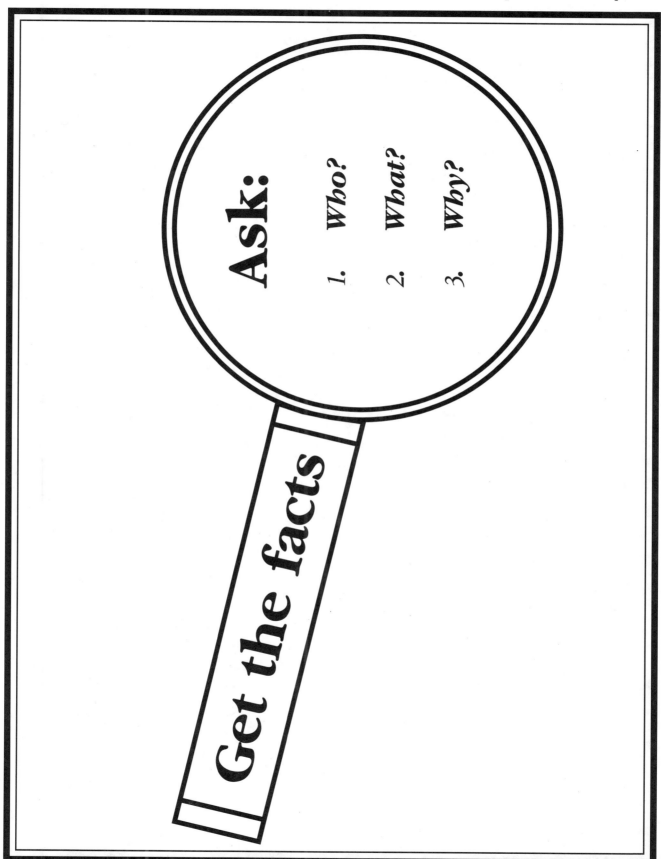

Ask:

1. *Who?*

2. *What?*

3. *Why?*

Get the facts

Jean Is Mean

An original story by Gwen Sitsch

Ellie had a best friend whose name is Jean.
Ellie now thinks that Jean is mean.

It all started just last week.
Ellie said "Good morning," but Jean didn't speak.

Ellie was sad; she didn't know
why Jean wouldn't even say "Hello."

At school she told her teacher Mrs. Fly
who told Ellie to ask Jean why.

But Ellie wouldn't talk to Jean.
She thought Jean was just too mean.

At recess Ellie wanted to play ball,
but Jean wouldn't include Ellie at all.

Ellie told her other friend and began to cry.
Her friend told Ellie to ask Jean why.

But Ellie wouldn't talk to Jean.
She thought Jean was just too mean.

On the bus Ellie saved Jean a seat,
but Jean sat next to a boy named Pete.

Ellie was mad at her friend Jean,
but she didn't want to cause a scene.

When she got home, she told her dad
about how Jean was acting so bad.

Dad could tell Ellie was about to cry,
and he told her to ask Jean why.

But Ellie wouldn't talk to Jean.
She thought Jean was just too mean.

So Ellie went outside to play,
and there was Jean. What should she say?

She remembered the advice of her teacher and dad
and decided that asking wouldn't be so bad.

"Jean, why have you been so mean today?
You won't talk or speak or play."

Jean looked Ellie right in the eye,
and Ellie thought Jean was about to cry.

"I'm angry at you," replied Jean.
"You're the one who has been so mean."

"Me? What did I do?
You're my friend. I couldn't be mean to you."

Jean said, "I heard it all from our friend Tess.
She said you said my writing was a mess."

Ellie smiled and said, "I didn't say mess.
I said your writing was the BEST!"

Jean smiled and hugged Ellie tight.
And then everything was just right.

JUMPING TO CONCLUSIONS

Grade Levels:
1–5

Purpose:
Students will be able to identify how jumping to conclusions before getting all the facts can lead to conflict.

Estimated Time:
20–25 minutes

Materials:
none

Procedures:
1. Discuss what it means to jump to conclusions. Emphasize that this involves deciding what has happened in a situation without getting all the facts. Have students give examples of times that they may have jumped to conclusions.

2. Read some of the situations below and have students tell what they immediately *THINK* has happened. Then read what really happened to the students. After each scenario, process how some of the ideas offered by the students could have led to a conflict.

3. Older students may enjoy writing some scenarios on their own and sharing with the class.

Examples:

You see two of your friends on the playground looking at you and laughing. What do you think is happening?

> **The true situation:** The friends see something funny going on behind you and are laughing at that.

You walk by the principal's office and see a classmate sitting outside the principal's office crying. What do you think is happening?

> **The true situation:** Your classmate has just been told that someone in his family has had an accident and he's waiting for his parents to come get him.

You can't find your new book that you just bought and someone in your homeroom is reading a book just like it. What do you think is happening?

> **The true situation:** You left the book in the reading center and your classmate did not know that it is yours.

You walk into a room where a lot of your friends are laughing and talking. When you enter, they all stop. What do you think is happening?

> **The true situation:** Your friends were planning a surprise party for you.

You see a special picture you drew for your teacher in the trash can. What do you think has happened?

> **The true situation:** The picture was in a stack of papers that your teacher threw away and she did not realize it was there.

DETECTIVE DRESS

Grade Levels:
1–3

Purpose:
Students will be able to identify all the necessary parts in finding the facts.

Estimated Time:
20–30 minutes

Materials:
Enlarged pictures on page 16

Procedures:
1. Remind students that getting the facts involves being like a detective. Discuss what a detective does.

2. Display the enlarged picture of the person in street clothes where it is visible for all students. Introduce the person as Darby the Detective. Ask if Darby looks like a detective and discuss why not.

3. Tell the students that you are going to give Darby some things that a detective needs and that each of these things will help Darby and them as they try to uncover facts when a conflict starts.

4. Place the detective's hat on Darby's head and emphasize that one thing that must be done when getting the facts is to *THINK*. Discuss how people must think of appropriate questions to ask, think about what they already know, and think about what they are seeing and hearing.

5. Place the magnifying glass in Darby's hand. Discuss how a detective must *LOOK AND OBSERVE* all the things that are happening. Relate this to trying to find the facts when a conflict may be starting.

6. Place the trench coat on Darby. Discuss how the trench coat covers almost all of Darby. Discuss how a detective must *COVER EVERYTHING* by asking questions when looking for clues. Relate how people must be sure that they've done all they can to find the facts.

7. Relate how to use all three parts in getting the facts first in a conflict. You may choose to discuss the scenario of someone bumping into you at the water fountain as presented in the initial lesson.

    Think: Tell yourself to slow down and not just react. Think of how to get the facts.

    Look and Observe: Turn and look at the person. Look at his or her expression and body language. Determine if you feel anything different is going on. Keep an open mind.

    Cover everything: Ask questions. Ask, "What happened?"

8. Summarize by pointing out the three things that a good detective does: think; look and observe; and cover everything.

9. You may choose to allow students to draw themselves as a detective with the three essential parts—the hat, the magnifying glass, and the trench coat.

Patterns for Darby the Detective

FACT FINDER

Grade Levels:
2–5

Purpose:
Students will be able to decide if given information is a fact and, if not a fact, will tell how to get the actual information.

Estimated Time:
20 minutes

Materials:
a card for each student with the word "FACT" on one side and "NOT" on the other (see page 19)

Procedures:

1. Review what it means to "get the facts." Emphasize that getting the facts includes seeing and hearing things for yourself as opposed to hearsay.

2. Develop a list of question words that could be used when trying to find the facts. This is easily explained by using the "5 Wh's and the H": who, what, when, where, why, and how. Write these words on a chalkboard or chart paper that is visible during the entire lesson.

3. Read a situation as given in the examples below or tell a similar situation. Have students decide if the given information justifies something that is fact. They will signal their response to you by holding up the appropriate side of their card.

   If the information given is not a fact, have several students explain how they would go about getting the facts by asking unaccusing questions. Refer to the question words listed on the board when necessary.

   You may also choose to discuss how a conflict could begin or become worse if someone were to act on a situation that is not a fact.

Examples:

You see a friend looking your way and laughing. You feel she is laughing at you. Is it a fact that your friend is laughing at you?

Your brother tells you that your best friend called you a name. Is it a fact that your friend called you a name?

You hear your classmate say that he thinks you have ugly shoes. Is it a fact that your classmate said this?

Your teacher smiles at your friend when she gives an answer but not at you when you give your answer. You think your teacher doesn't like you. Is it a fact that your teacher doesn't like you?

You see your classmate next to you looking in your direction and writing down answers. Is it a fact that she is cheating from your test?

Your friend teases you when you get a "C" on your math test. Is it a fact that your friend is teasing you?

Your sister comes into your room and takes your favorite CD. Is it a fact that she has your CD?

Your new pencil is missing and someone in your class is holding one just like it. You say that it is yours. Is it a fact that the pencil is yours?

Your brother was the last person to have the remote control and now it is missing. You tell your mom that he lost it. Is it a fact that your brother lost the remote control?

You think that you turned in your homework but your teacher does not have it. You tell your friend that your teacher lost your homework. Is it a fact that your teacher lost it?

FACT

NOT

TALK SHOW

Grade Levels:
3–5

Purpose:
Students will be able to ask questions to discover the true reason behind a conflict.

Estimated Time:
30 minutes

Materials:
pretend microphone

Procedures:

1. Set up the front of the classroom like a stage. Have the "talk show guests" sit in chairs facing the class who is the audience.

2. Prior to class, discuss the plot of the conflict with the "talk show guests" (you may choose one of the examples listed below). You may get as detailed as you like about how you would like the guests to answer the questions. Be sure that the "guests" understand that they are only to answer the question asked and not to elaborate on any question. Emphasize giving just the facts.

3. Discuss the "5 Wh's and the H" question words. These include who, what, when, where, why, and how. Write these words on a board visible to all students.

4. You may act as emcee of the "talk show." Ham this up as much as you like. For example, you may want to begin with, "Good afternoon, ladies and gentlemen. Welcome to 'You Get the Facts' where our audience's job is to help find the reason a conflict has begun. As you recall, our studio audience asks the questions of our guests. Let me introduce our guest to you today." At this point proceed with giving some sketchy detail as to the dilemma going on with the "guests."

5. Using your microphone, have students take turns asking the "guests" questions that may uncover what has actually happened to cause the conflict. The questions must begin with one of the Wh or H words listed on the board. Emphasize that the question cannot be a guess as to what has happened such as "Did she take your comb?"

6. When the allotted time for asking questions is over, each member of the "audience" is to write down his/her hypothesis as to what the conflict is about. Then tell them the real situation and process how those who guessed correctly arrived at their answer. Also process incorrect guesses and how the "audience" arrived at their hypotheses.

Examples:

Tell the audience this: *Jamal and Erica used to play together every day after school. Now they don't and both are hurt and angry. Please welcome Jamal and Erica to our show.*

> **The real conflict:** Jamal's brother, Robert, teased him about playing with a girl. Now Jamal thinks that if he plays with Erica, his brother and his brother's friends will tease him more.

Tell the audience this: *Linda and Shauna are not speaking to each other. They are both friends with Laci, who is not on our show today. Linda and Shauna have never really been close friends but now they act as if they hate each other. Please welcome Linda and Shauna to our show.*

The real conflict: Linda told Laci a lie about Shauna that made Laci mad at Shauna. Shauna found out what Linda told Laci and then told Laci that if she was friends with Linda she couldn't be her friend anymore. The girls are really jealous of the relationship the other has with Laci.

Tell the audience this: *Ralph and Ed worked on a science project together and did not win a prize. Since the judging, they have been arguing over everything. Please welcome Ralph and Ed to the show.*

The real conflict: Ed told everyone in the class that Ralph's dad did all of Ralph's part and that Ed did all the hard stuff.

Take a Polaroid picture but do not let the students see what you are shooting. As the picture develops, have students keep watching it and trying to guess what it's going to be. Be sure that they notice that it gets clearer and clearer. Explain that you have to wait for the whole picture to become clear to know for sure what it is. Emphasize how students jumped to conclusions when the picture was still fuzzy.

Play the "gossip" game or "telephone line." Whisper a sentence to one person who in turn whispers to another, and so on. The person at the end says aloud what they thought they heard. It's interesting to see how much the information can get turned around. This becomes a good example of how information gets distorted when it is passed from one person to another. Stress the importance of going to the original person involved to get the facts.

Take a close–up picture of one part of a large item or do an overlay on a picture with a small opening cut to expose part of the picture. Have students guess what it really is. Emphasize how you cannot base a judgment on just part of what you see.

MADNESS MANAGEMENT

Grade Levels:
1–5

Purpose:
Students will be able to: tell appropriate ways to express anger; identify three guidelines for madness management; identify "fouls" in conflict situations; and explain why "fouls" are inappropriate.

Estimated Time:
30–45 minutes

Materials:
- *Coping With Conflict* poster
- MADNESS MANAGEMENT mini-poster
- 1,2,3. . . card (see page 25)
- mouth card (see page 25)
- (optional) reproducible MADNESS MANAGEMENT mini-poster for each student (see page 26)

- a referee s
- a ball
- a whistle
- a backpack
- 3 or 4 heavy stones
- (optional) a puppet

Procedures:

1. Review the last lesson. If you used a puppet in your previous lesson, have the puppet come back and report that he or she did go to the other student to get the facts and that the student said he or she did not like her and told her to "Buzz off!"

2. Discuss how we feel when we have conflicts. Emphasize that anger is a natural feeling we have when we are in a conflict situation. Stress that anger is an okay feeling to have, but that what people <u>do</u> with their anger is very important. Point out the next section on the *Coping with Conflict* poster, MADNESS MANAGEMENT. Explain that this means being in control of mad or angry feelings.

3. Explain the three rules for handling anger: 1) you may not hurt yourself; 2) you may not hurt someone else; and 3) you may not hurt property.

4. Emphasize not hurting yourself as holding in feelings without doing something to get them out, or without dealing with them. This could be demonstrated by having a child put on a backpack and placing heavier and heavier stones in it until the weight of the backpack becomes almost unmanageable. Then ask the child how he/she would do in a soccer game while holding that heavy backpack. Explain that if people carry their angry feelings around inside them, these feelings interfere with everyday life.

5. Tell students that they must be aware of a trap that they can fall into when they are angry. Put on the referee shirt and whistle and discuss the role of a referee in a game—to be sure everyone plays fair and that no one fouls.

6. Explain fouls in conflict situations as those things we say or do that hurt someone else.* Emphasize that oftentimes when we are talking about angry feelings we may foul by saying things that hurt the other person. Give examples of fouls that we may do while talking (name–calling, blaming, teasing, bossing, etc.).

7. Explain the other kind of foul as something we do that hurts another person's body. Have students give examples (hitting, pushing, shoving).

8. Ask students whose responsibility it is to be the referee when they are having a conflict with someone else. Emphasize that each person is in control of his/her own behavior and therefore must be his/her own referee.

9. Explain that instead of fouling when we are angry, we need to find appropriate ways to deal with our feelings. Show the 1, 2, 3 . . .card. Explain that counting to 10 slowly is one way of taking time to release angry feelings. Model counting to 10 to calm down and have students practice.

10. Tell students that sometimes when people are angry they feel a need to do something because they have lots of energy. Bounce the ball and show how this helps to get anger energy out. Have students suggest other ways of getting anger energy out. Emphasize that it does not have to be an outdoor activity. If not brought up, suggest drawing or playing a musical instrument.

11. Show the picture of the mouth. Tell students that talking about angry feelings is an appropriate way of managing madness. Have students name people they could talk to about their angry feelings. Emphasize that talking to the person with whom you are angry is not a good idea at this point.

12. Encourage students to follow the rules of MADNESS MANAGEMENT and to find appropriate ways to deal with their madness. Display the MADNESS MANAGEMENT mini-poster outside the MADNESS MANAGEMENT section on the *Coping With Conflict* poster.

13. Distribute copies of the reproducible MADNESS MANAGEMENT mini-poster to students. (optional)

*The concept of "fouling" is adapted from *The Rules for Fighting Fair*, Grace Contrino Abrams Peace Education Foundation. Reprinted with permission ©1996. All rights reserved.

1, 2, 3. . .

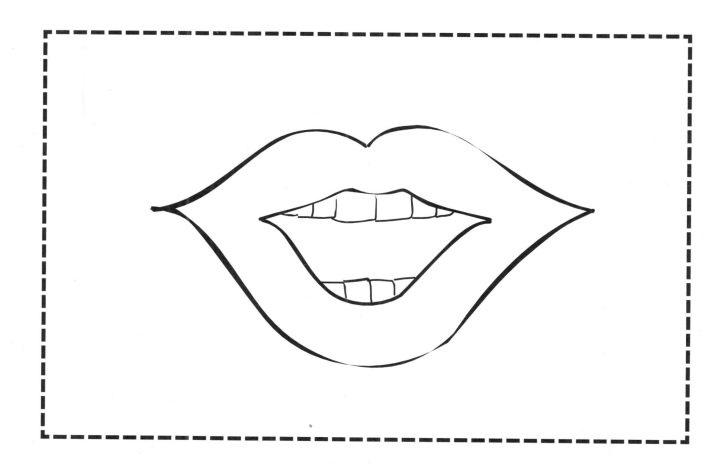

Madness Management

You may choose to:

1, 2, 3 . . .

Stop and count to 10

Talk with someone about your anger

Do something to let out your anger energy

Rules:

1. You may not hurt yourself.
2. You may not hurt property.
3. You may not hurt someone else.

- Calling Names
- Teasing
- Threatening
- Bossing
- Bullying
- Making Excuses
- Hitting or Shoving
- Getting Revenge

No Fouling

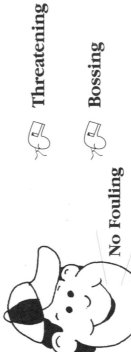

TEMPERATURES RISING

Grade Levels:
1–5

Purpose:
Students will be able to identify ways to "cool down" conflict situations.

Estimated Time:
20–30 minutes

Materials:
- construction paper fire flames pattern (see page 28)
- thermometer pattern (see page 28)
- paper ice cubes pattern (see page 28)

- suggestions for cooling down (see ice cube messages on page 29) taped to plastic ice cubes that can be placed in a freezer and frozen (these may be purchased at discount stores)

Procedures:

1. Display the construction paper fire flames, thermometer, and ice cubes. Ask students what these symbols might mean. Explain that people sometimes say and do things that "heat up" a situation and make it worse. It is helpful to know ways to "cool down" situations.

2. Read the conflict situation as given in the example below. Have students point out the fouls in the situation. Write these on the flames.

   You are getting ready to do your writing assignment and you look for your pencil. It's not in your desk and you're almost certain that you left it there. You look at the other kids in your class working and notice that a classmate of yours is using a pencil just like the one you left inside your desk. Angrily you go over to your classmate and say, "You little thief. Give me back my pencil right now. I know that you took that out of my desk." Your classmate looks at you and continues to work. You say, "If you don't give me that pencil right now, I'll get you at recess." Your classmate replies, "If you weren't such a scarecrow brain you could keep up with your things. You're always losing things. I found this on the floor." "Well, it's mine! Now give it to me right now or you'll be sorry," you reply. Your classmate throws the pencil across the floor and says, "Fine, if you want it, you go get it." The pencil breaks and no one gets to use it.

3. Have students think of ways that the situation could have been cooled down. Write these on the ice cubes.

4. Discuss how difficult it can be when another person seems to be fouling you, but explain that each person has a responsibility to do what he/she can to cool down a situation that has the potential to become worse. When a conflict arises, ice cube thoughts can help cool down the situation.

5. Take out the bowl of plastic ice cubes that have the ice cube messages taped to them. Throw these out to students and have them read the messages aloud. Discuss how each may help cool down a conflict.

6. You may choose to display a set of construction paper ice cubes in the room with the ice cube messages written on them to serve as a reminder to students.

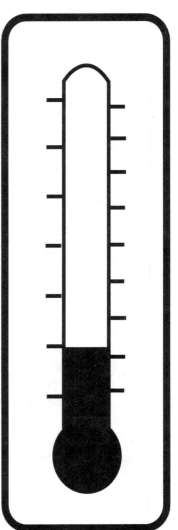

Ice Cube Messages

Let's not foul. It will only make the conflict worse.	Let's share.	Let's take turns.
I'm sorry.	Let's talk about this later when we're both calm.	We can work out this conflict.
We're making too big a deal of this.	Let's talk it out.	We can get help.
Let's flip a coin to see who goes first.	I'm willing to work out a compromise.	I don't want to fight with you.

Magnets

Grade Levels:
1–5

Purpose:
Students will be able to identify things they say that create conflicts or things they may say that help avoid conflicts.

Estimated Time:
15–20 minutes

Materials:
• a set of magnets   • chart paper

Procedures:
1. Show a set of magnets. Demonstrate the two reactions that can occur when you put magnets together. Ask what is happening. Summarize that magnets can either attract one another or repel each other.

2. Explain that this often happens with people. The things we say and do can either attract others to us or repel others away from us.

3. Have students give examples of things people may do to repel other people. These may include calling names, arguing, putting others down, or disrespecting. Write these ideas on a chart entitled "Repellers" to be displayed in the room.

4. Have students give examples of things people may do to attract others to them. Ideas may include saying "Hello," picking up something someone drops, holding a door for someone, or smiling at others. Write these ideas on a chart table entitled "Attractors" to be displayed in the room.

5. Emphasize that when conflicts occur, madness can sometimes lead us to do things that repel others. People watch us at all times, so it is important to always be in control of yourself so that you do not accidentally repel others.

TOUCHDOWN

Grade Levels:
3–5

Purpose:
Students will be able to identify fouls and describe ways to manage conflicts without fouling.

Estimated Time:
20 minutes

Materials:
- a paper penalty flag for each student (see pattern page 32)
- story, *Fouls, Fouls, and More Fouls* (see page 33)

Procedures:

1. Discuss that the goal of conflict management is to find appropriate ways to handle the everyday conflicts or problems that arise. Relate the game of football or soccer to the game in life of handling conflicts. In football, a team tries to reach the goal. The best way to do this is to think clearly, avoid fouling, and make good choices. In life, when conflicts occur, the goal is to handle them well. This is best accomplished by thinking clearly, not fouling, and making good choices.

2. Give each student a paper penalty flag. Instruct them to hold up the flag each time they hear a foul in the story you are about to read to them and to identify the foul.

3. Read *Fouls, Fouls, and More Fouls.*

4. Discuss the story and brainstorm ways the conflict could have been managed without fouling.

Fouls, Fouls, and More Fouls

An original story by Diane Senn

Brandon was in math class completing his work when his pencil lead broke. Brandon got up to sharpen his pencil, and as he walked between the desks, he accidentally stepped on Justin's new paperback book that was on the floor beside his desk. Justin had just bought that book with his own money from the school's book fair.

Justin yelled, "Hey, get off my book. You should be careful, you big jerk!'

Brandon did not mean to step on his book, and he did not like being called a name. Brandon replied, "It was an accident. It's your fault anyway for being so messy with your books. That was dumb of you to leave it on the floor."

Justin retorted, "Well maybe you need to get those funny looking glasses fixed so you can see better. Is your family too poor to get good glasses?"

Brandon pushed at Justin and said, "Hey, you leave my family out of this."

The teacher heard the disturbance and sternly said, "Boys, there doesn't need to be any talking. Brandon, you need to be in your seat."

Brandon reluctantly returned to his desk with a grim look on his face.

Justin was really mad inside as he thought to himself, "How dare he push me! He can't do that. Just wait; I'll get even with him at recess!"

During that morning neither student did his best work. Their minds were thinking about how mad they were about what had happened and about what was said. They each spent their time thinking about what they were going to do to get back at the other.

Later that morning the class went to lunch. At lunch, Justin passed Brandon in line and whispered in a low voice, "I'll get you back at recess. You better watch out!" Justin sat with some of his friends and told them that he did not like Brandon and that he was mad at Brandon. Justin asked his friends to help him "get" Brandon.

When recess arrived they lined up to go outside. Outside, Justin, with his friends, went over to Brandon, who had also rounded up some of his friends. Justin went up to Brandon and said, "How dare you push me in class! Nobody pushes ME around!"

"Oh yeah, you're not so tough," said Brandon as he shoved Justin to the ground. Justin pushed Brandon back and a crowd gathered. At that moment the teacher on recess duty blew the whistle at Brandon and Justin. Both boys were sent to the office for the choices they made about their behavior.

MADNESS MONSTERS

Grade Levels:
1–3

Purpose:
Students will be able to identify sources of anger and ways to control anger.

Estimated Time:
20 minutes

Materials:
Play–Doh® or modeling clay for each child

Procedures:

1. Give each student a blob of Play–Doh® or modeling clay. Ask them to think of something that causes them to feel angry. Ask them to make a "Mad Monster" out of their clay that represents their mad feelings or actions.

2. Have students share what they have made. Caution them that in their sharing they may not foul someone. For example, a child would not be allowed to say, "John makes me mad because he thinks he is so smart." (Note to teachers: ALL mad feelings are acceptable as long as students do not foul someone while sharing these feelings. Never say, "You should not feel . . .")

3. Discuss how all people have "Mad Monsters" in their lives. These are the things that "get under our skin" and make us feel anger. Emphasize that "Mad Monsters" grow and grow if we do not keep them in control.

4. Have the students reshape their monsters into something they could do when they are angry. Give examples such as a jump rope, a musical instrument, a crayon, a mouth to talk it out, or ten pieces of the clay to represent counting to ten. Be sure that many different ideas are explored to include physical activity, artistic activity, and talking.

5. Allow students to share what they did with their clay. If inappropriate ways are shared, be sure to process why the method is not acceptable and to offer alternatives.

6. You may discuss other ways to deal with anger such as scribbling on paper, writing down what you are mad at, or sharpening a pencil. Another way to control anger is the "Turtle Technique." When a person feels his anger getting out of control, he can act like a turtle and "pull in" - take time to think. Then when he is back in control, he can come out and deal with the situation.

SNOWBALLING

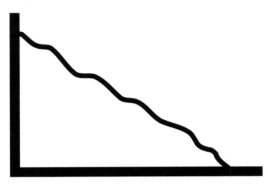

Grade Levels:
1–5

Purpose:
Students will be able to identify the damage fouls do to conflicts.

Estimated Time:
20 minutes

Materials:
a large white piece of paper cut in the shape of a downhill slope

Procedures:

1. Ask students to offer their thoughts on why fouls are inappropriate and what fouls do to conflict situations.

2. Display the downhill slope in a place that is visible to all students. Tell the students that you are going to show them what fouls do to conflicts.

3. Have the students name as many fouls as they can think of. Write these on the cut–out of the downhill slope.

4. Ask students to pretend that what you have created is a mountain that is covered with snow. The fouls stand for the snow. Show them a very small white ball (this can be a piece of paper). Tell the students that this small snowball is going to represent a conflict. Explain that the conflict is a small one such as a problem with someone sitting in your seat.

5. Ask the students to predict what would happen if you took a small snowball and rolled it down a snow–covered slope. Relate this to rolling that very small conflict you just discussed in fouls. Explain that when you make a choice to foul someone you make the conflict larger and larger with each foul.

6. Have students think of examples of times when a conflict they had got larger because of fouling. You may choose to have students write or draw about a time this happened to them.

Additional Ideas
Madness Management

Give each student a piece of bubble gum. Discuss the importance of "chewing on a problem" rather than "chewing out" someone. Discuss what it means to "chew out" someone and how it can make a conflict worse. Emphasize the importance of putting efforts and energy on finding appropriate ways to solve a conflict.

Locate stories in the local newspaper that indicate how uncontrolled anger and fouling made a conflict worse. Brainstorm positive alternatives to handling the situation.

Discuss how hard it may be at times not to foul someone when they have fouled you. Emphasize the importance of making appropriate choices about personal behavior rather than reacting to someone else's behavior. Demonstrate with a marionette puppet how we do not need to let someone else "pull our strings" and simply react, but that we can choose not to foul back.

Discuss that life sometimes hands us a tough situation. Use the example of someone being angry at us or fouling us. Explain that it is often helpful to turn the situation around and add some kindness or goodness to the situation. Demonstrate this with a lemon. Squeeze a lemon and ask the students how the juice will taste. Then add sugar to the lemon juice and ask how it might taste now. Relate this to tough situations. Discuss ways to "add the sugar" to a problem instead of fouling.

Grade Levels:
1–5

Purpose:
Students will be able to model caring listening skills and use an "I" message.

Estimated Time:
30–35 minutes

Materials:
- *Coping With Conflict* poster
- CARING COMMUNICATION mini–poster
- (optional) Puppet
- (optional) reproducible CARING COMMUNICATION mini-poster for each student (see page 41)

Procedures:
1. Review the previous conflict management skills taught.

2. Explain that often when conflicts occur it is difficult to know what to say or do. Explain that today's lesson will focus on how to communicate with someone else in a conflict situation.

3. Point out CARING COMMUNICATION on the *Coping With Conflict* poster. Define communication to students emphasizing the two roles—speaker and listener.

4. Discuss the role of the listener first. Role play with a puppet or a student appropriate and inappropriate listening skills.

    ROLE PLAY ONE: Have a student or the puppet tell you a story about his/her favorite movie. You look away and ignore. Stop the scene and get feedback on what's wrong. Emphasize the importance of **eye contact.** Replay again and look at the speaker while he or she is talking. Discuss.

    ROLE PLAY TWO: Have another student or the puppet tell you about his/her most fun relative. Fold your arms and use a bored look. Stop the scene and discuss. Emphasize the importance of **body language**. Active listening body language may include nodding the head, turning the body toward the speaker, arms uncrossed, sitting still, and a pleasant facial expression. Replay the scene and use appropriate body language as the student or puppet talks.

    ROLE PLAY TWO: Ask another student or the puppet to tell you about his/her favorite place to visit. You interrupt with your favorite place to visit. Stop the scene and discuss. Emphasize the importance of listening and not just waiting for your turn to talk. Explain that others know we're listening when we **say something back** that shows we were listening. Replay and use reflective listening skills.

5. Discuss the role of the speaker. Emphasize that it is often difficult to talk with someone when there is a conflict because what we say and the way we say it can sometimes make a conflict worse. Teach the "I" message using the steps given. Set up a situation where a girl named

Margaret is always taking your glue from your desk. Work through this with the steps as outlined below:

> *Say the person's name. . .* "Margaret,"
> *Tell the person how you feel. . .* "I feel mad. . ."
> *Tell the person why. . .* "when you take my glue without asking."
> *Tell the person what you want beginning with the word "please". . .* "Please ask first."

6. Give situations and have students practice sending an "I" message using the formula given above to someone who is to practice using appropriate listening skills. Examples may include:

   - Someone who always cuts in front of you when the teacher is not looking
   - Someone who taps his pencil on his desk when you're trying to work
   - Someone who walks away from a game when she doesn't get her way
   - Someone who grabs the book you've chosen to read

7. Caution students that "I" messages seem to work best when talking to a friend or someone who is not intentionally trying to bother you. "I" messages are a nice way of letting others know that what they are doing is not pleasing you.

   "I" messages may not work if someone is trying to bully you. The intent of a bully is to make you feel bad. Tell the students that the next lesson will give some ideas to help if an "I" message does not work.

8. Display the CARING COMMUNICATION mini-poster outside the CARING COMMUNICATION section on the *Coping With Conflict* poster. Review with the mini-poster.

9. Distribute copies of the reproducible CARING COMMUNICATION mini-poster to students. (optional)

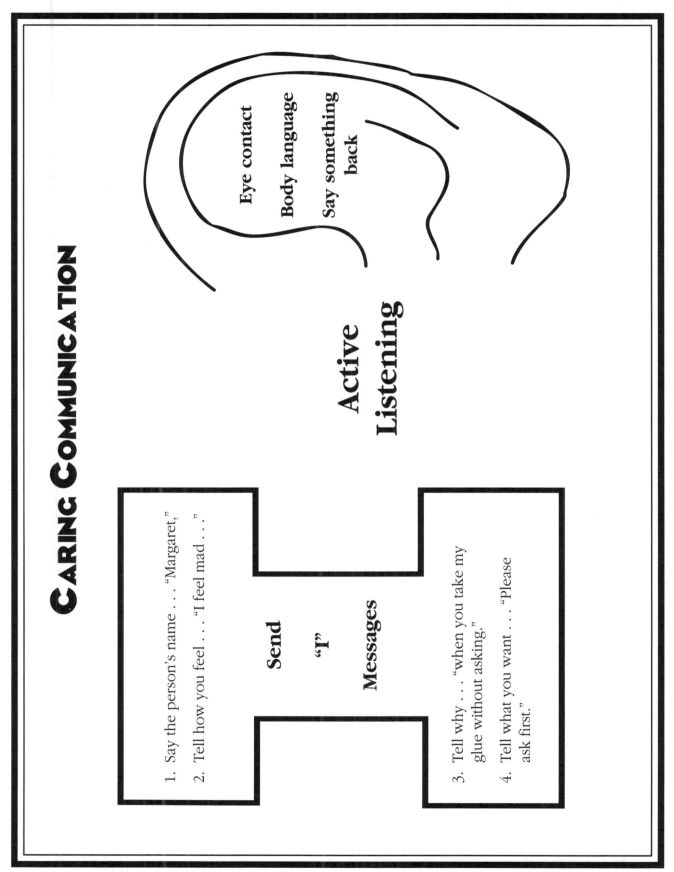

CARING COMMUNICATION

Active Listening

Eye contact

Body language

Say something back

Send "I" Messages

1. Say the person's name . . . "Margaret,"
2. Tell how you feel . . . "I feel mad . . ."
3. Tell why . . . "when you take my glue without asking."
4. Tell what you want . . . "Please ask first."

HEART TO HEART

Grade Levels:

1–5

Purpose:

Students will be able to model sharing the role of listener and speaker in communicating during a conflict.

Estimated Time:

20–25 minutes

Materials:

heart–shaped pillow (see page 43 for directions)

Procedures:

1. Explain to students that when a conflict occurs the people involved may have a "heart to heart" talk. During a "heart to heart" talk, the people involved discuss their feelings about the conflict by exchanging "I" messages and using active listening skills.

2. Review the steps in sending an "I" message and the steps in active listening. These are to be used when having a "heart to heart" talk.

3. Show the heart–shaped pillow. Explain that the pillow will be kept in your class and can be used to help students have "heart to heart" talks. It is a way of structuring a talk where both can discuss their feelings about a conflict.

4. Explain the guidelines for using the pillow as outlined below:

    A. Each person takes part in the talk. The person holding the pillow talks first. The talker's role is to say an "I" message. The role of the listener is to use active listening skills. After the first person has spoken, the pillow is passed to the other person who then assumes the role of the talker.

    B. Each person gives suggestions to solve the conflict.

    C. Choose from the suggestions given how best to solve the conflict.

5. You may choose to use these more formal guidelines:

    • Both people must agree to solve the problem.
    • No fouls.
    • Each person takes a turn talking. Do not interrupt.
    • Be as honest as you can without hurting feelings.

6. Allow students to practice having a "heart to heart" talk with the pillow. Make up some simple conflict situations or use the ones given in the CARING COMMUNICATION supplemental lesson "Role Playing."

"Heart to Heart" Pillow Pattern

To make a heart-shaped pillow, use the pattern below and enlarge to the size needed (approximately 15" in length and width). Use red material, poly-fill stuffing and lace. Cut the material to the enlarged pattern, stuff, and sew.

LISTENING PAIRS--APPLES AND ORANGES

Grade Levels:
3–5

Purpose:
Students will be able to practice appropriate active listening skills and discuss how they feel when others do not listen.

Estimated Time:
30 minutes

Materials:
- two sets of paper apples for half the class with the instructions "Ignore" and "Show you don't care with your body" (see page 45)
- paper oranges for the other half of the class with the instructions "Change the subject when I'm done" written on them (see page 45)

Procedures:
1. Divide students into pairs. Designate one person in the group as an apple and the other as an orange.

2. The apples receive a paper apple with the instructions "Ignore" written on it. Instruct the apples not to allow the oranges to see their apple.

3. Have the oranges talk about a specified topic for one minute. The apples are to follow the instructions on their apple.

4. Discuss what happened after the minute is over. Ask the oranges what they wanted from the apples. Emphasize the importance of eye contact when someone is talking.

5. Reverse roles. Give the oranges their orange with the instructions "Change the subject when I'm done." Ask the apples to talk for one minute about a specified topic. At the end of the one minute tell the apples that the oranges will respond to what they said.

6. Discuss the importance of saying something back that shows you were listening to the other person.

7. Reverse roles one more time with the apples receiving the instructions "Show you don't care with your body." Have the oranges talk for one minute. Following the minute, discuss how body language can interfere with listening.

8. Allow the pair to each talk one more time. Have the listener use appropriate active listening skills.

9. Discuss how it feels when someone listens to you when you talk as opposed to someone who does not listen.

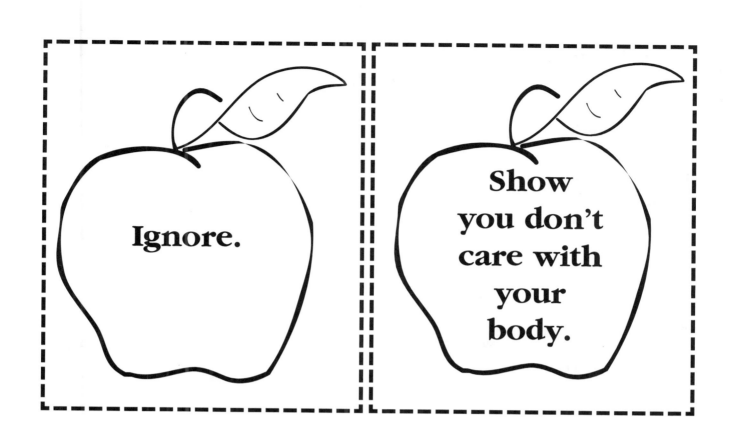

Ignore.

Show you don't care with your body.

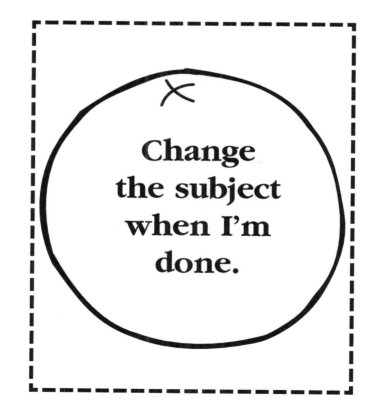

Change the subject when I'm done.

BODY TALK

Grade Levels:
1–5

Purpose:
Students will be able to identify how body language affects communication.

Estimated Time:
30 minutes

Materials:
none

Procedures:

1. Review the steps in CARING COMMUNICATION. Emphasize how body language is as important as what a person says with his/her mouth. Demonstrate this by saying the same thing twice but with a different look. Look at someone, smile and say, "Nice shirt." Then repeat the words but roll your eyes when you say it. Discuss the difference in the two statements.

2. Point out that there are some "blockers" when it comes to communication. Discuss the message sent by each of the following "blockers":

   folded arms   *hands on the hips*
   furrowed eyebrows   *rolling eyes*
   tightened lips

3. Discuss that there are also some communication "enhancers." Explain that the word "enhance" means to make better. Discuss the message sent by the following "enhancers":

   smiling   *eye contact*
   nodding your head   *widened eyes*

4. Ask students to "say" the following things to the class without using any words. You may write these on slips of paper and have the class guess what is being said with body language:

   "I'm disappointed in you."   *"I'm interested in what you're saying."*
   "That's a dumb idea."   *"I feel very angry right now."*
   "That's a great idea!"   *"I'm sad."*
   "You're in big trouble."   *"I'm bored."*

5. Reemphasize that the goal in CARING COMMUNICATION is to talk and listen in a respectful way and that body language is of great importance in modeling this respect.

FEELINGS VOCABULARY

Grade Levels:
1–5

Purpose:
Students will be able to identify words that express various feelings.

Estimated Time:
15–20 minutes

Materials:
chart paper

Procedures:
1. Review the steps in CARING COMMUNICATION. Emphasize that in order to send an "I" message, a person must express his/her feelings.

2. Make a face that looks angry. Ask students to identify as many words as they can that would express the feeling you are modeling. Write these on the chart paper.

3. Model a sad expression. Repeat the above procedure.

4. Repeat the same procedure for a happy expression.

5. Display the chart in the classroom so that students have a feelings vocabulary readily available. Encourage the students to add other feeling words as they think of them.

6. If you have time available you may allow students to choose a certain feeling and model this. Allow the class to guess the feeling that is being modeled.

Sample Feelings Vocabulary

angry	upset	furious	excited
frustrated	mad	tense	surprised
worried	bothered	sad	shy
happy	confused	lonely	relieved

ROLE PLAYING

Grade Levels:
1–5

Purpose:
Students will be able to model appropriate CARING COMMUNICATION skills.

Estimated Time:
20–25 minutes

Materials:
"I" messages Role Play Cards (see pages 49-50)

Procedures:
1. Review the skills involved in being an active listener: eye contact, body language, and reflective listening.

2. Review why and how to send an "I" message. Be certain that students know all four steps in sending an "I" message: say the person's name, tell how you feel, tell why, and tell what you want.

3. Have students take a role play card and read the situation. Choose someone to be the listener. Have the speaker and listener model appropriate CARING COMMUNICATION skills. Allow the class to give feedback as to how the speaker and the listener modeled the CARING COMMUNICATION skills.

"I" Messages Role Play Cards

Your friend Thomas always tells your secrets to other people in your class. This bothers you. What could you say?

Your little brother Henry always gets into your room and messes it up. What could you say?

Julie is singing and you'd like her to be quiet so you can read. What could you say?

You are still painting your picture and your friend Martha takes the yellow paint. You're not done with it. What could you say?

Kay, who sits next to you, always bumps you. This bothers you. What could you say?

Wendy took the only pen on your desk. What could you say?

Your sister Marie always seems to be tying up the telephone. You need to make a call. What could you say?

You are doing your work and your friend Shannen keeps asking you questions. It is keeping you from getting finished. What could you say?

You are working on a science project with Ralph and he is not doing his part. What could you say?

Gary took your pencil without asking. What could you say?

You answer your teacher's question wrong and your friend Amy, sitting next to you, laughs at you. What could you say?

Nancy and Mary are playing together at recess and you join them. Nancy begins to boss you around. What could you say?

Your friend Marcus says he won't play with you anymore if you play with the new boy John. What could you say?

You're at home reading a book when your brother Rob comes along and wants to read the same book. He pulls it out of your hands. What could you say?

You get a new pair of glasses and your friend Ronald starts to tease you. This bothers you but you don't think Ronald realizes that. What could you say?

You are lining up for lunch and Billy cuts in front of you. What could you say?

You are in class trying to do your seatwork and Arthur keeps making noise with his pencil. What could you say?

Suzi didn't do her homework and wants to copy yours. When you say "no," she gets mad. What could you say?

Each time you need your scissors it seems that Joey has them. What could you say?

George sits next to you and always has his books on your desk. What could you say?

Gina always seems to interrupt you when you are sharing a story. What could you say?

Additional Ideas
Caring Communication

Give the BIG EAR AWARD (see page 52) to students that you see modeling active listening skills. You may choose to hand students the certificate or you may choose to display a picture of a large ear on a bulletin board or wall and allow students to write their names on the big ear when you catch them being appropriate listeners. If you have a big rubber ear (available at party costume or novelty stores), children love wearing this for a given time in the classroom to show that they have been big listeners!

Include feeling words as a part of a classroom spelling or vocabulary list. You may choose to have one comfortable and one uncomfortable feeling included each week. This encourages students to use feeling words other than simple ones such as mad, sad, and glad.

Play "I'm going on a picnic." You begin by saying, "I'm going on a picnic and I'm going to bring . . ." Say something you're going to bring. The next person says "I'm going on a picnic and I'm going to bring. . ." That person must first say what you have said and then add what they are going to bring. Play continues with each person naming all the previous items before adding his/her item to the list. This encourages appropriate listening skills.

Relate listening to using a hearing aid. Explain the various functions of a hearing aid: turning the volume up to hear people better, adjusting the volume to screen out background noise, or turning the aid off so that you are not disturbed. Ask students to describe times that using the functions of a hearing aid may be important. For example, sometimes it's important to turn the volume up to listen better such as when a teacher is giving directions.

"The Big Ear Award"

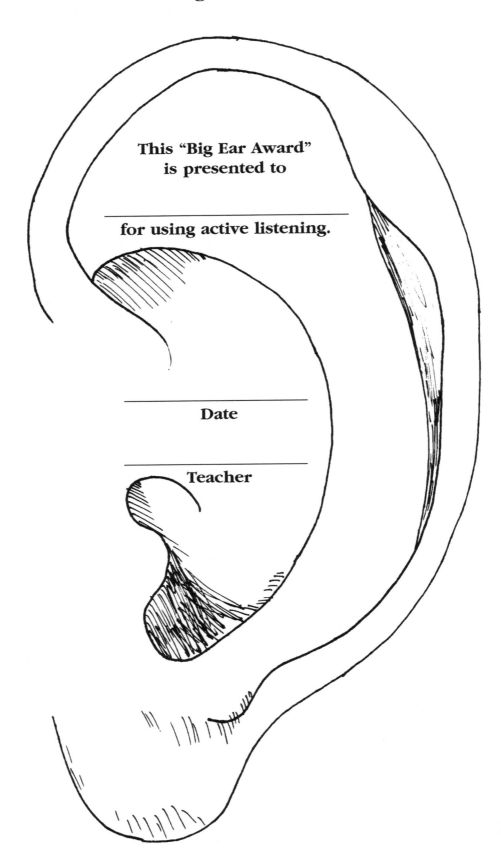

This "Big Ear Award"
is presented to

_____

for using active listening.

_____
Date

_____
Teacher

Grade Levels:
1–5

Purpose:
Students will be able to identify 12 strategies for solving conflict.

Estimated Time:
30–45 minutes

Materials:
- *Coping With Conflict* poster
- TIMELY TOOLS mini-poster
- hammer
- Timely Tools box (see pages 55-84)
- (optional) reproducible TIMELY TOOLS mini-poster for each student (see page 54)

Procedures:
1. Review the previous skills. Explain that these skills alone will many times help manage a conflict but that sometimes, even after these skills have been tried, the conflict may still exist.

2. Show the hammer. Tell students you are going to build a house and say that you have everything you need because you have a hammer. Cajole them until they say that there are other things you will absolutely need to build your house. Bring out the importance of having the right tools for the job.

3. Explain that in conflicts, different things may need to be done to manage the conflict. As in building a house, the right tool is essential to get the job done.

4. Show the Timely Tools box. Go over each "tool" in the box. As you discuss each, have students offer suggestions as to conflicts where the tool you are discussing may be the appropriate one to use. The tools are:

IGNORE	AVOID
SHARE	TALK IT OUT
TAKE TURNS	NEGOTIATE
COMPROMISE*	APOLOGIZE
GET HELP+	HUMOR
POSTPONE	CHANCE

5. Present several conflict situations and have students choose a tool that may "get the job done." Emphasize that there may be several "tools" that may be appropriate.

6. Review the TIMELY TOOLS mini–poster and display the mini-poster outside the TIMELY TOOLS section on the *Coping With Conflict* poster.

7. Distribute copies of the reproducible TIMELY TOOLS mini-poster to students. (optional)

*Caution students that they never compromise if someone is trying to talk them into doing something they feel is wrong.

+Adult intervention is always appropriate if students are being harmed or feel they may be harmed. Be sure to emphasize that students always use this tool first if someone is hurting them.

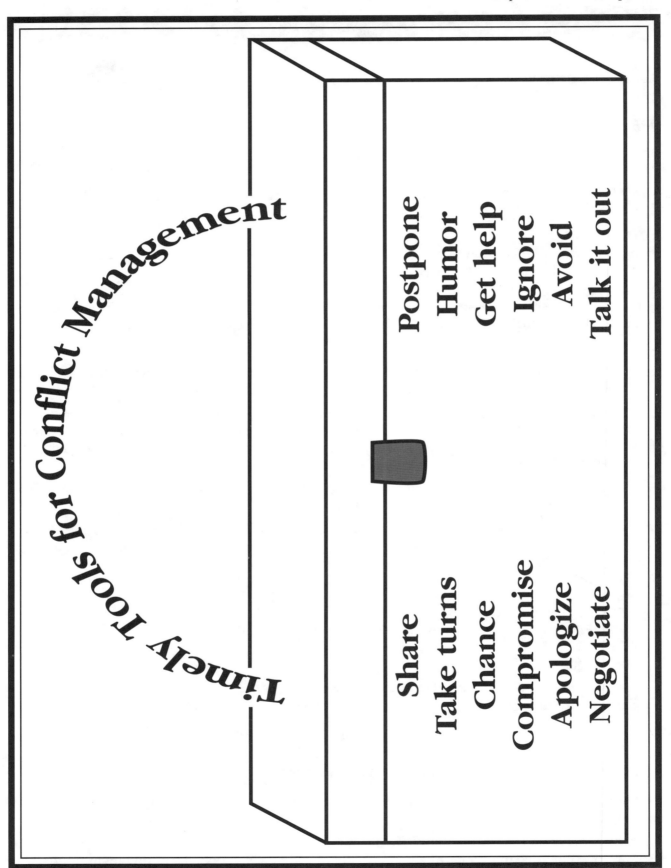

Timely Tools for Conflict Management

Postpone
Humor
Get help
Ignore
Avoid
Talk it out

Share
Take turns
Chance
Compromise
Apologize
Negotiate

Directions for Making Your Timely Tools Box

Items for the Timely Tools box include:

- Timely Tools box label (see page 56)
- Directions for use (see page 56)
- Copy of the *Coping With Conflict* poster card with "Managing Conflict" questions (see pages 57 and 58)
- 12 Timely Tools cards (see pages 59-82)
- Role Play cards (see pages 83-84)
- A small resealable plastic bag
- Some type of box that resembles a tool box. We used plastic detergent canisters (we found Rubbermaid® detergent canisters work well). Other suggestions are to spray paint used detergent boxes with handles, use gift bags or use resealable gallon plastic storage bags. (If using the bag, change the wording from Timely Tools box to Timely Tools bag!)

Steps:

1. Reproduce the Timely Tools box label and Directions for Use. Cut and attach to the tool box.

2. Reproduce the *Coping With Conflict* poster card page on one side of colored cardstock and "Managing Conflict" on the reverse side. Place in tool box.

3. Reproduce the 12 Timely Tools cards front and back (visual on one side, explanation on the other) on a different color card stock than the poster card. Tool cards can be reproduced and used as they are or additional items may be attached to the tool cards for added visual appeal (see below). Place in box.

   Additional items to attach to tool cards (optional)

TAKE TURNS:	thin dowel for see saw
CHANCE:	die (one per card)
IGNORE:	two cotton balls and one pipe cleaner for the earmuffs
TALK-IT-OUT:	two hearts on pink and red construction paper or cardstock cut and attached
COMPROMISE:	rope tied together and attached
NEGOTIATE:	highlight steps in yellow
SHARE:	plastic cookie in half
POSTPONE:	reproduce stop sign on red cardstock and attach
APOLOGIZE:	bandage
HUMOR:	add color to the clown
AVOID:	attach black yarn around the ⊘
GET HELP:	white fabric or paper cut into the shape of a flag with SOS written on it and a thin dowel glued for the flag pole

4. Reproduce role play cards on cardstock. Cut, put in a small resealable plastic bag, and place in the Timely Tools Box.

(Reproduce, cut, and attach to the outside of the Timely Tools Box.)

TIMELY TOOLS BOX

Directions for Use

(Reproduce, cut, and attach inside the Timely Tools Box.)

TOOL BOX:

USED TO FIX PROBLEMS AND TO BUILD RELATIONSHIPS

Instructions:

1. Choose the poster card and answer the questions.

2. Choose the right tool or tools for your conflict or problem.

3. Try it.

4. Think back over to see if the tool or tools worked well for the conflict.

COPING WITH CONFLICT POSTER CARD

MANAGING CONFLICTS

Ask yourself these questions before choosing the tools:

1. Did you get all the facts?

2. Is your madness under control?

   Are you thinking clearly and responsibly?

   Are you making sure not to foul--not to call names, tease, push, etc.?

   Remember, fouls only make the conflict worse!

3. Are you listening well to the other person?

   Are you sending an "I" message rather than a blaming message?

Choose one or more Timely Tools from the tool box that you think would be a helpful way to manage your conflict.

Take Turns

TAKE TURNS

When playing on a see–saw, the fun only happens when you take turns going up and down. Often a conflict can be solved by taking turns with each person having their way for a while. In doing this each person is happy.

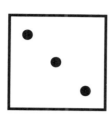

Roll the dice

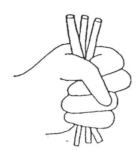

Draw straws

Flip a coin

Draw ideas or names from a "hat"

Hands on the bat

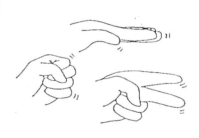

"Paper Rock Scissors"

Chance

CHANCE

When both of you have a disagreement over who goes first or whose suggestions or ideas to go with, you may choose to let chance or luck decide. Before "flipping a coin" or "drawing a straw" both of you must agree to accept the answer.

IGNORE

Just like a pair of earmuffs can block out the cold or block out a noise, sometimes it can be important to block out or IGNORE if someone is picking on you or teasing you. Sometimes people may pick or tease just to get you mad or upset. If you choose to ignore them and get busy doing something else, this may manage the problem.

HEART-TO-HEART

Talk-it-out

TALK-IT-OUT

A heart can remind us of loving and caring about others. So when you have a problem, have a "heart–to–heart" and talk about your feelings in a caring way. Be sure each person has a chance to talk and listen.

Compromise

COMPROMISE

A rope could be used in a tug–of–war with each side pulling in a different direction working against the other. One side wins and the other loses. Conflict is not solved this way. Instead, we could take both ends of a rope and willingly come together to form a circle; both become winners. In compromise, both can stop pulling in their opposite directions and decide to work together.

Negotiate

NEGOTIATE

Dealing with a conflict or problem with someone is like walking stairs
. . . we must take it one step at a time.

Step one: Say what the problem is.

Step two: Brainstorm together all the possible ways to handle the
problem (write these down if it helps).

Step three: Think of the good and bad consequences of each idea you
came up with.

Step four: Together choose a way to handle that is O.K. with each of
you.

Step five: Do it.

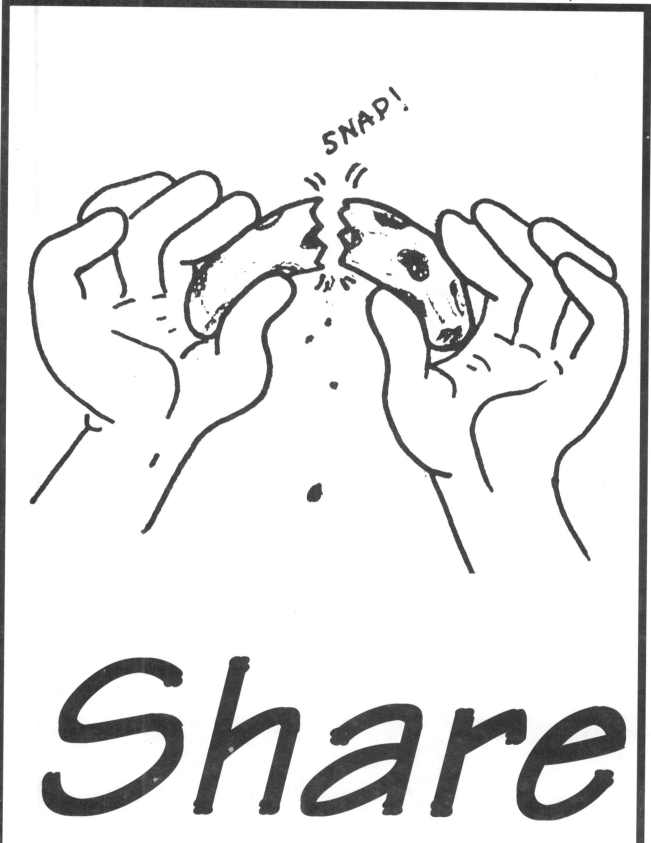

SHARE

If two people are hungry and only one cookie is available, a conflict could arise. Sharing is a way to work through a conflict. If both people want the same thing it can often be shared, and both people end up happy with the way things worked out.

Postpone

POSTPONE

A stop sign tells a driver to stop, look both ways, wait until all is clear, and then go on when it is safe. When you have a conflict with someone and one or both of you become angry or tired——STOP, put off dealing with the conflict until another time when you have cooled down and can discuss it.

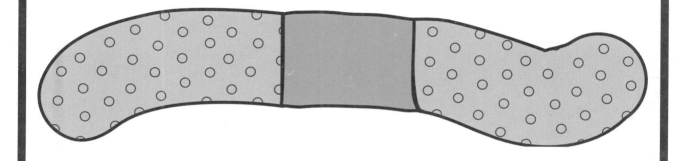

Apologize

APOLOGIZE

Just like a bandage can help when you scrape your knee or leg, an apology, saying "I'm sorry," can help when someone gets hurt from a conflict or disagreement. Say "I'm sorry" if you did something wrong. If you feel you did not do anything wrong, it can still help to say, "I'm sorry that we have gotten into this argument."

Humor

Humor

Just as a clown can bring the laugh or humor to a situation at the circus, sometimes we can look at our problems with a little humor or laugh and not take all of our problems so seriously. It is important not to laugh AT the other person but to laugh WITH them or at the problem.

AVOID

There are situations that may be dangerous. For example, there may be someone that always picks on you or gives you a hard time. Therefore, you may need to avoid that person or stay away from them so there will not be a problem.

S.O.S.

Get Help

GET HELP

Just like an S.O.S. flag is a signal flag calling for help when a boat is in distress, we often get in distress with conflicts. This could happen when you have tried many ways to settle the conflict and have been unsuccessful or if someone is about to be hurt. GET HELP. Go to a person who can be counted on for a fair decision in helping to solve the conflict such as a teacher, parent, counselor, grandparent, or someone else that you can trust.

Reproducible Timely Tools Role-Play Cards

You want to play a game and your friend says that if you don't jump rope she's going home. What could you do?

You and your friend are playing a game and you both want to go first. What could you do?

Someone on the bus calls you names every day. What could you do?

Your aunt gives you and your brother $10 together to spend at the toy store. You want one thing and your brother wants another. What could you do?

Your friend let you borrow his new crayons and now you can't find them. Your friend is upset. What could you do?

You saw your friend cheat to win the game you're playing, but your friend denies it. What could you do?

Your sister won't clean her side of the playroom. Your parents have said that no one can watch TV until the playroom is clean. What could you do?

Your grandma is coming to town for the day. Your best friend has invited you over for the same day. You know that your friend's feelings have been hurt when you've not been able to come over before. What could you do?

You have asked your brother many times not to touch your new CD. Now it is missing and he says he doesn't know anything about it. What could you do?

You checked out a book from the media center and your little sister scribbled in it. What could you do?

Your best friend is saying mean things about the new kid in your class. She says that if you're friends with the new girl you can't be her friend. What could you do?

When your friend comes over to play with you, she always leaves your room a mess and then you have to clean it up. What could you do?

You are with a group of your friends who are planning a class party. Every time you start to say something you get interrupted. What could you do?

Some tough kids in school seem to do a lot of picking on others. Out at recess, they are playing on the basketball court. You usually like to play basketball or soccer at recess. What could you do?

You and your brother both want to sit in the front seat of the car, but there is only room for one. What could you do?

Mary just pushed you while walking down the hall. What could you do?

You are trying to do your math homework. Your sister has the TV turned up so loud that you can't think. What could you do?

You are trying to listen to the teacher, but your friend keeps talking to you. What could you do?

Your friend is visiting at your house for the afternoon. Your friend wants to play outside and you want to play video games. What could you do?

You're watching a favorite TV show when someone changes the channel. What could you do?

At recess, you join a group playing soccer. As you're playing, they start to make fun of you by laughing at the way you're kicking the ball and saying that you're no good. What could you do?

A kid you know calls you names. What could you do?

GROUP VACATION

Grade Levels:
3–5

Purpose:
Students will be able to work out conflicts using the timely tools.

Estimated Time:
30 minutes

Materials:
Timely Tools box

Procedures:

1. Review each of the Timely Tools by taking them out of the Tool Box and displaying them where they are visible to all students.

2. Divide the class into groups of no more than five students each (four students per group works best).

3. Explain to the students that they are going to make a group decision. Everyone in the group must agree upon the answer. Each task will have a specified time limit (you decide on the time limit). If the group has not agreed in the time limit, they must return to the previous task while the other groups get another task.

4. Give the tasks specified below one at a time. Remember to set a limit on how much time the group has to decide each. At the end of the time, have the groups tell you their decision by responding in unison. If someone does not respond, be sure that you check to see that they agree on the answer given by the group.

5. Let each group share how they came up with their answer pointing out if there were any group conflicts. If a conflict occurred, ask the group which tool they used to handle it. The most frequently used tools for this activity include compromise, chance, talk it out, and taking turns.

Tasks:

Your group has won an all expenses paid vacation to anywhere in the world. Where are you going?

Decide how you are going to get there.

You may take only one adult chaperon with you. It can be any adult in the world. Who will it be?

You may bring back one souvenir. It must be able to fit inside a suitcase. What will it be?

TOOLING TOGETHER

Grade Levels:
3–5

Purpose:
Students will be able to relate conflict management "tools" to everyday conflicts.

Estimated Time:
30 minutes

Materials:
Timely Tools box

Procedures:

1. Divide the class into groups of no more than five students.

2. Give each group three Timely Tools cards. Instruct the group to make up a conflict that could be solved using all three of the cards given. If you choose, students may be instructed to write the conflict down. You could use the examples in other lessons.

   Recommended groups: ignore, avoid, get help

                            chance, take turns, share

                            talk–it–out, apologize, negotiate

                            compromise, postpone, humor

3. When each group has finished, have the group act out their conflict and the ways it could be managed.

4. Have other students decide if any of the tools their group has could also be used to work out the conflict presented by other groups.

TOOL SORT

Grade Levels:
3–5

Purpose:
Students will be able to identify strategies that may help manage a given conflict.

Estimated Time:
30 minutes

Materials:

- Timely Tools box

- three large cards for each student with the words YES, MAYBE, and NOT! (see page 88)

Procedures:

1. Review the strategies for managing conflicts from the Timely Tools box.

2. Read a conflict situation (see examples below). Hold up a Timely Tools card and have students signal their response: YES, MAYBE, or NOT! depending on how they feel the strategy would apply to the given conflict.

Examples:

You get home from school and are very hungry. You go to the freezer and your brother arrives there at the same time. You both really want the last popsicle.

You are playing at your friend's house and he's being very bossy. He gets mad if you will not do everything exactly as he likes it.

Your classmate who is sitting next to you keeps making a cat noise and your teacher has called you down because she thinks it is you. Your classmate thinks it is funny and is doing it again.

You have been invited to your friend's birthday party, but your family has planned to go out of town. Ever since you told your friend that you would not be able to come, she has been ignoring you at recess and you think that she is mad.

All of your friends play tag at recess but you do not really like tag. This has led to teasing from some of the tag players.

YES

MAYBE

NOT!

CHOOSE THE TOOL

Grade Levels:
1–3

Purpose:
Students will be able to recognize the 12 strategies for managing conflicts.

Estimated Time:
20–25 minutes

Materials:
- Timely Tools box
- 12 index cards for each student or a set of small tool cards reproduced for each student (see pages 90-91)

Procedures:
1. Review each of the Timely Tools. As you are reviewing the 12 tools, have each student write the strategy on an index card and place it on his/her desk, or use the reproduced cards. Display the Timely Tools cards so that all students can see them.

2. Make up a conflict and end the scenario with the conflict being managed using one of the timely tools but do not give the word that tells the outcome. Have students hold up the small tool card that says what strategy was used to manage the conflict. Examples may include:

    Janet and Tracy wanted to play a game. They agreed on the game but could not agree who would go first. They both wanted to go first. They decided to draw straws to see who would go first. Which Timely Tool did they use?

    Marcie and Rosita could not agree on a science project. They really wanted to work together. Marcie wanted to do the science project on the solar system. Rosita wanted to do it on plants. They thought and thought and finally decided that since they both liked the ocean they would do the science project on ocean life. Which Timely Tool did they use?

    Robert was always being bothered by Charles. Charles called Robert names every chance he got. Robert felt really bad, but he decided that he would not let Charles know that he felt bad. Every time Charles called Robert a name, Robert pretended not to hear Charles. He wouldn't even look Charles' way. Which tool did Robert use?

| CHANCE | COMPROMISE |

| SHARE | NEGOTIATE |

| TAKE TURNS | POSTPONE |

90

HUMOR

GET HELP

AVOID

TALK-IT-OUT

IGNORE

APOLOGIZE

PARENT INFORMATION

Introduction

Communicating your program to parents is one of the most important things you can do. Not only does communicating the program with parents keep them informed of what is being taught, but it also gives them the opportunity to reinforce the conflict management skills at home with their children. Students' success in retaining these skills is increased when the skills are not only being taught and reinforced at school but also being reinforced at home.

You may choose to do more involved conflict management skill training with parents. However, the following materials provide information to the parents about what is being taught in the program and encourage them to reinforce the skills at home. This section presents two ways to share the material in the *Coping With Conflict: An "Elementary" Approach* program with parents. One is through parent letters sent home with students following each initial classroom lesson. The second is through information about the program being published in a school newsletter. This section contains articles that you may publish in your school newsletter. The articles provide general information on conflict management as well as information on each specific skill in the program.

You may reproduce the articles and letters from this book provided that you cite the book.

CONFLICT MANAGEMENT

Turn on the television or read a newspaper and chances are you will see or read about violence in our society. Some startling statistics have been released recently:

- *By the age of twelve, the average child has witnessed 8,000 murders and 100,000 acts of violence on TV or movies.*
- *Nearly 60% of 2,058 students surveyed in grades 6–12 reported that they could quickly get a handgun if they wanted one.*

Conflict in and of itself is not bad. Conflicts arise naturally because of the uniqueness of people. People make choices about how to handle conflict and these choices can lead to inappropriate acts against others. Many experts support the idea that teaching conflict management skills to children may help alleviate some of the acts of violence that are being committed by children today. Therefore, we have recently begun implementing a conflict management program in our school.

Our program centers on four skills that help children learn to work out conflicts in a peaceful way. These skills include:

FACTS FIRST
MADNESS MANAGEMENT
CARING COMMUNICATION
TIMELY TOOLS

Your child will be learning these skills in classroom lessons. Teachers and staff schoolwide will be reinforcing the skills through classroom activities as well as assisting students in using the skills when a conflict arises.

Conflict management skills are important in families too. Conflicts arise on a daily basis in family situations between various members in a family. For the next several weeks information in the school newsletter will focus on the conflict management skills your child is learning. It is our hope that you will reinforce these skills in your home as you deal with family conflicts.

CONFLICT MANAGEMENT: FACTS FIRST

When conflicts arise in families (as they often do), people often jump to conclusions. We assume we know the facts when we may not actually know everything. One of the first things we can do to keep a conflict from becoming any larger than it already is, is to get the **FACTS FIRST**.

This is done by asking non–accusing questions. As parents, we so often ask questions thinking that we already know the answer. Many times we have tried and convicted our children before we take the time to listen.

Parents may worry that the act of being Judge and jury will lead to children being untruthful. This can be avoided by having the facts first rule in your home. This simply means that everyone in the family understands the importance of telling the truth when conflicts happen. Praise honesty.

Many times gathering the facts can solve the conflict. Often when we discover that something was not as it seemed, the conflict is over. Help your child practice the facts first rule by modeling this for your child.

CONFLICT MANAGEMENT: MADNESS MANAGEMENT

Good people never get angry, right? WRONG! Anger is a normal emotion just as happiness and sadness are. However, we often get upset with ourselves or our children for being angry. Anger is not bad—it's the choices that we make in handling anger that can lead to trouble.

Helping your children learn to manage their madness is appropriate no matter what age your child is. You can use the three rules about **MADNESS MANAGEMENT** in your home:

1. It is not okay to hurt myself.
2. It is not okay to hurt someone else.
3. It is not okay to hurt property.

Give your children appropriate "outs" when they are angry. Encourage them to do something to let out their anger energy or to talk to you about their feelings. This skill is best taught by modeling. Show your children what you do to constructively release your anger such as exercising or engaging in a favorite hobby.

A trap that everyone can fall into when they are angry is "fouling." Fouls are those things that are said or done that hurt someone else's feelings or their body. Fouls cause conflict to escalate. Some examples include: calling names, teasing, getting revenge, bossing, threatening, making excuses, hitting or shoving, and bullying. Students are encouraged to think of themselves as their own referee in order to control their own personal fouling.

Fouls attack the dignity of the people we love. They cause feelings of resentment, hatred, and revenge. They can destroy family relationships. Recognize fouls and work together as a family to eliminate them.

CONFLICT MANAGEMENT: CARING COMMUNICATION

It is difficult to listen when your feelings are hurt. However, listening is essential to understanding a problem and healing a hurt. We all tend to look at only our side of a conflict. It is imperative to use active listening.

Active listening consists of many things. First, make eye contact with the person who is talking. Second, hear what the person is saying. Third, use some type of reflection to let the person know you're listening. This may include nodding your head, saying "uh–huh," or repeating what the other person has just said. Last, check your body language. Are you scowling? Are your arms folded?

Another part of caring communication is using an "I" message. The opposite of this is a "YOU" message. "YOU" messages tend to blame, judge, boss, or threaten. These messages cause others to become defensive. An "I" message has four parts:

Say the person's name.
Tell the person how you feel.
Tell the person why you feel that way.
Tell the person what you want.

An example of an "I" message is, "Mike, I feel frustrated when you don't clean your room after being asked to do so. Please have your room clean by 4:00 today."

It is also important to choose an appropriate place and time for discussion. If the time at hand is not adequate, schedule a time and place for a talk. Bad timing can actually start a conflict.

CARING COMMUNICATION lets the people you love know that they are important to you and respected by you. Modeling this type of communication goes a long way in teaching your child.

CONFLICT MANAGEMENT: TIMELY TOOLS

Often when conflicts surface it may be difficult to know exactly what to say or do to make the situation better. It is helpful to know strategies ahead of time that may be used to manage conflicts. As all conflicts are different, strategies used must be different. It is important to choose the strategy or "tool" that best addresses a specific conflict.

You may find it helpful to brainstorm strategies for coping with a conflict when it arises in your family. Let everyone involved in the conflict work together for ideas and avoid any preconceived solutions.

The **TIMELY TOOLS** that may be helpful in working out a conflict include:

- compromise+
- talk-it-out
- share
- postpone
- ignore
- humor

- chance (flip a coin, draw straws)
- take turns
- negotiate
- avoid
- get help*
- apologize

+ Children need to be taught that there are times they NEVER compromise. These times may include when someone is trying to get them to do something they know or feel is wrong.

* Children should be taught that if they are being hurt, they always get help first. They should never try to deal with a conflict if they are in danger.

Your attitude toward conflict goes a long way in teaching your child to deal with it. Do not be afraid to laugh at yourself. Look upon conflict as a way to grow together and learn more about each other!

Dear Parent,

Today in class we began a series on managing conflict. The program is entitled *Coping With Conflict: An "Elementary" Approach.* The program focuses on teaching students what a conflict is and on four guidelines for managing conflict in a peaceful way.

The program utilizes a *Coping With Conflict* poster as well as a Timely Tools box to focus on the following skills:

1. **FACTS FIRST.** Emphasis is placed on understanding the conflict or problem before jumping to conclusions.

2. **MADNESS MANAGEMENT.** Students are taught ways to manage any anger that may result from the conflict situation before trying to handle it. They are cautioned about "fouls." Fouls in conflict situations include those things that are done either intentionally or unintentionally to hurt the other person(s) involved in the conflict. Some examples include name calling, teasing, hitting, pushing, blaming, making excuses, and bullying. Emphasis is placed upon the fact that fouls tend to make conflict situations even worse. Madness management techniques include counting to ten, doing a physical activity to release anger energy, and talking to someone uninvolved about the anger.

3. **CARING COMMUNICATION.** Students are taught communication skills that help facilitate working out a conflict. These skills include listening and sending an "I" message to the other person(s). "I" messages communicate to the other person how what they are doing is making you feel. "I" messages take the place of "you" messages which tend to blame the other person and put them on the defensive.

4. **TIMELY TOOLS.** Each class will be equipped with a conflict management Timely Tools box. Included in this box will be 12 ideas for working out conflicts. Examples include talking it out, compromising, taking turns, sharing, avoiding, and getting help. Look for more detailed information about the tool box in an upcoming letter.

Today's lesson focused on what the word *conflict* means and on skill number one: **FACTS FIRST**. Please ask your child what a conflict is. Conflict was defined for them as a problem that needs to be worked out with another person or persons. Many children refer to this as a fight or an argument. I would like students to understand that arguments or fights may result from conflicts not being managed, but that conflicts themselves are the problems that cause people to disagree. Some conflicts can be avoided by simply getting the facts rather than jumping to false conclusions.

It may be beneficial to use some of these same guidelines in your home when it comes to handling conflicts that arise. If you would like more information on the program or would like to view the *Coping With Conflict* poster or Timely Tools box, please call me.

Sincerely,

Dear Parent,

Today we continued our study of conflict management. If you recall, we recently began our study of conflict management skills. The previous lesson focused on defining what a conflict is as well as the first skill for handling a conflict—finding out the **FACTS FIRST**. Students learned to ask questions before assuming they knew the cause of the conflict.

Today your child learned the second skill for conflict management--**MADNESS MANAGEMENT**. Students learned that when conflicts happen the involved persons usually feel anger and that anger in and of itself is not a "bad" thing. It's how people handle anger that is important. We discussed ways of handling anger such as counting to 10 before reacting, doing a physical activity such as bike riding or running to reduce anger energy, and talking to someone uninvolved in the conflict about angry feelings. Students learned three rules for managing madness: 1) I may not hurt myself; 2) I may not hurt other people; and 3) I may not hurt property.

Students were cautioned about "fouls." In games, fouls are things that are against the rules. In a conflict situation, a foul is something that is done that puts the other person down or makes him feel badly about himself. Some fouls include teasing, calling names, bullying, blaming, making excuses, and physical acts such as hitting or shoving. Students recognize that fouls only make a conflict worse. Students are encouraged to think of themselves as their own referee in order to control their own personal fouling.

Since conflict is part of everyday life, students benefit from learning that there are ways to handle it appropriately. It is my goal that students learn and practice these conflict management skills now so that they become a part of their encounters with others.

Sincerely,

Dear Parents,

Our third lesson in the series on conflict management was today. As you will recall, students have learned two skills thus far for peaceful conflict management: **FACTS FIRST** and **MADNESS MANAGEMENT.** Today's lesson focused on **CARING COMMUNICATION** skills.

Students learned that there are two roles in communication—the speaker and the listener—and that each role is very important. The role of the listener in **CARING COMMUNICATION** is threefold: to maintain eye contact, to use appropriate body language, and to say something back that shows he/she was listening. Active listening is often the most overlooked skill in communicating, and not listening can escalate conflicts.

The role of the speaker in **CARING COMMUNICATION** is to send "I" messages. An "I" message lets the other person know how you are feeling and why without blaming or fouling. An "I" message has four parts:

1) Say the person's name. . . "Becky,"

2) Tell the person how you feel beginning with the words "I feel". . . "I feel mad. . ."

3) Tell the person why. . . "when you take my pencil without asking."

4) Tell the person what you want beginning with the word "please". . . "Please ask first."

We practiced **CARING COMMUNICATION** by role playing different conflicts that may occur. Both the speaker and the listener roles were emphasized as important. We also discussed how this technique may not work in certain situations such as when someone is teasing or bullying. The purpose of teasing or bullying is to make another person feel badly. Therefore, telling the person how you feel is generally ineffective. Other techniques will be presented for dealing with teasing or bullying in another lesson in our series, **TIMELY TOOLS**.

Sincerely,

Dear Parents,

The last skill in our series on conflict management was taught today. You will recall that students have learned three skills to date: **FACTS FIRST; MADNESS MANAGEMENT;** and **CARING COMMUNICATION**. Today's skill is **TIMELY TOOLS**.

Just as choosing the correct tool is essential to getting a job done, choosing an appropriate "tool" or strategy in a conflict is essential in getting the conflict settled peacefully. Our class has a "tool box." This is a collection of different strategies that students may use to work out conflicts they have with others. "Tools" included in the **TIMELY TOOLS** box are:

POSTPONE: A person may choose to put off working on the conflict especially if one or both persons is angry or tired.

AVOID: There are situations and/or people who can and should be avoided.

IGNORE: A person may choose not to get involved or to not let something become a conflict for him/her. This can prevent a conflict from getting worse.

APOLOGIZE: Say "I'm sorry" if you did something wrong. If you did nothing wrong, you may say, "I'm sorry we're having this conflict."

COMPROMISE*: Sometimes both sides can give in a little and meet in the middle.

CHANCE: Flip a coin, draw straws, or any other such luck device.

HUMOR: Never laugh at someone, but you may laugh at a conflict if it is no big deal.

SHARE: Find a way for all to use or enjoy together.

TAKE TURNS: Allow each to have a turn in order to be a part and enjoy.

NEGOTIATE: Problem–solve by thinking of all the possible choices and deciding on one upon which both people can agree.

TALK IT OUT: Have a "heart to heart" where feelings are discussed in a caring way.

GET HELP[+]: If a conflict is escalating, it is sometimes necessary to seek the help of a trusted adult.

Each of these strategies is written on a card and paired with a visual to help students relate to the meaning of the "tool." I welcome you to come in and see the Timely Tools box.

It has been a pleasure teaching these conflict management skills to your child. It is my hope that with the efforts of home and school together, our students learn to deal with conflicts peacefully.

Sincerely,

*Students have been cautioned to never compromise if someone is trying to convince them to do something they feel is wrong.

[+]Adult intervention is always appropriate if children are being harmed or feel they may be harmed. Students have been instructed to use this tool first if someone is hurting them.

PUPPET SHOWS

Using the Scripts

This section of the book contains scripts that can be used for puppet shows. There is a script for each skill area taught in the *Coping With Conflict* program in addition to an introductory script that familiarizes students with the superhero CM. CM stands for Conflict Manager.

Each script is written for not more than three puppets. There are follow–up questions following each script that can be used to stimulate discussion of the information presented in each script.

You may use the scripts in a number of ways. You may wish to have selected students in your classroom perform the shows for the entire class. Older elementary students may perform the shows for younger elementary students as a reinforcement of the skill areas. Or you may choose to have students act out the skits instead of using puppets.

If you use puppets, we suggest having students tape record their voices first and then perform the show using the taped script. This makes the show flow better and is easier for children to understand and follow.

Puppet Show One
CM TO THE RESCUE

Summary: Students meet CM, Conflict Manager, and learn the meaning of the word conflict.

CM: Hi, boys and girls. I'd like to introduce myself to you. My name is Conflict Manager or CM for short. You see the letters CM on my shirt. My job is to help people when there's a conflict. (*Pause*) What's that you're saying? You don't know what a conflict is? Oh, well, let me back up and explain.

A conflict is when people have a problem with each other. Everyone has a conflict with another person from time to time. You may be able to think of a time that you were having a problem getting along or agreeing with someone. That was a conflict. Most times conflicts happen with people that we are really close to—friends, brothers or sisters, or classmates.

Some people call a conflict a fight, but a conflict is different from a fight. Fights may happen if people choose not to handle conflicts in a peaceful way. I do not like fights. My job as a superhero is to be sure that people know how to handle conflicts in a peaceful way.

I'm going to fly around now and see if I spot a conflict going on. You watch and see if you can recognize a conflict.

CM flies away and two other puppets, Deb and Carline, come on stage. CM stays off stage for now.

DEB: Hey, Carline, want to play a game?

CARLINE: Sure, how about playing pogs?

DEB: Naw, I don't want to play pogs. I really want to play jacks.

CARLINE: Well, I don't like jacks. Besides pogs are more fun.

DEB: No they're not. Jacks is the coolest game there is.

CARLINE: No way! Jacks is boring.

DEB: Is not.

CARLINE: Is too.

DEB: Not.

CM flies in.

CM: Wait!

CARLINE: Who are you?

CM: I'm Conflict Manager or CM for short. I see you've got a conflict going on here.

DEB: Huh?

CM: A conflict. It looked to me from up there in the sky that you two are having a problem agreeing about what game you are going to play.

CARLINE: Yeah. I want to play pogs but she wants to play jacks.

CM: That's a conflict. My job as super CM is to help people see what their conflicts are and then to be sure that people are working the conflicts out in a peaceful way.

DEB: Gee, CM, I'm glad you came when you did because we were really starting to get mad at each other.

CM: I stopped you this time, but it is important for you to be able to stop yourselves when you have a conflict because I'm not always around to do it for you. Remember, when you start to have a problem with someone, stop yourself and say, "Hey, we're having a conflict here. Let's be sure that we work this out in a peaceful way."

CARLINE: Thanks, CM. You're really smart! How can we work this out?

CM: Look at the *Coping With Conflict* poster in your classroom at school. There may be some ideas there.

DEB: We have one in our class. Let's go now and see if there's an idea on that poster to help us. Thanks, CM!

CM: You're welcome. I'm off now to be sure that conflicts around our school are being managed in a peaceful way. So long for now!

Follow-up Questions for Puppet Show One
CM TO THE RESCUE

1. What is a conflict?

2. Give an example of a conflict that you've had with someone else.

3. What is CM's job?

4. What was the conflict in the puppet show?

5. Since CM cannot be everywhere there is a conflict going on, what is your responsibility when you have a conflict with someone else?

Puppet Show Two
DEB GETS THE FACTS

Summary: Deb learns how jumping to conclusions can lead to conflict.

Puppet named Deb is alone on the stage and addresses the audience.

DEB: Hi, boys and girls. I'm sitting here inside during recess while the rest of my class is outside. Want to know why? I'll tell you about what happened today at recess.

I have this really good friend name Carline and we always play together. We tell each other all our secrets. Carline knows everything there is to know about me. We've been friends ever since we were three years old. I THOUGHT Carline was my friend—that is until today on the playground.

There's this new girl at school name Cynthia. She's okay, I guess. She used to live in Washington, D.C. so she has seen lots of neat things like the White House and the Lincoln Memorial. One day she brought pictures of some of the things in Washington, D.C. and she let me hold them. She answered questions I had like, "Does Abraham Lincoln's ghost really haunt the White House?" and "What does the president eat for breakfast?" I think she might have made some of it up, but that's okay.

Like I said, I THOUGHT Cynthia was okay—until today. After lunch we went to recess like always and I headed for the big rock that Carline and I always sit on at recess to talk. I always beat Carline there because my class finishes lunch first. So anyway, I'm just sitting there waiting on Carline when I see her coming out. Only she's not alone; she's with Cynthia, the new girl. I didn't think too much about it because like I said, Carline and I ALWAYS sit on the rock and talk during recess, so I just knew that Carline was coming over to talk. Only she didn't. She and Cynthia headed over to the monkey bars and started playing. Carline didn't even look my way. Then I saw Cynthia and Carline whispering to each other and laughing. I just knew that they were talking about me. I got so upset I told the teacher that I didn't feel good and she let me come inside.

I've just been sitting here thinking about what happened and I've made a plan. The next time Carline tries to talk to me, I'm just going to ignore her. That'll teach her. I don't think I even want to be her friend anymore. I never really liked her anyway. Oh, here comes Carline now. Well I'll just show her.

CARLINE: Hi, Deb. Whatcha doing sitting in here?

Deb makes no response.

CARLINE: Deb, didn't you hear me? I'm talking to you. Why are you sitting in here?

Deb turns away.

CARLINE: Deb, is something wrong?

Deb continues to ignore.

CARLINE: Fine, just be that way. I don't need you for a friend anyway.

Carline walks away off stage.

DEB: See, I showed her. She can't mess with me. Now I feel... well I feel...well, I thought I'd feel better but I don't. I feel just awful now. Carline is really mad at me now. Oh, what a mess this is!

CM flies in!

CM: Looks like there's a problem here.

DEB: Oh, CM, I'm glad you're here. I've just gotten into a big mess with my very best friend Carline. You see, Carline didn't come over to talk to me on the playground like she does every day and I saw her whispering to the new girl, Cynthia, and I just knew that they were talking and laughing about me. So when Carline came in a little while ago and tried to talk to me I just ignored her. She got really mad and left. Now I don't have a best friend anymore and I feel terrible.

CM: Sounds to me like you didn't remember the very first thing you always do when you think a conflict may be starting with another person.

DEB: What's that?

CM: Get the facts first. That means before you make up your mind about what happened, go ask questions to be sure that what you think was happening is what was really happening. Have you stopped to think that perhaps Cynthia and Carline weren't talking about you? Could they have been talking and laughing about something else?

DEB: Well, I guess they could've been talking about something else. But why didn't Carline come over to the big rock to meet me like she always does?

CM: Only Carline can answer that. I think you need to ask her.

DEB: Thanks CM, I think I will. You sure are a big help.

Both CM and Deb go off stage. Carline comes on stage alone and then Deb comes to join.

DEB: Hi, Carline. I know you might be pretty mad at me for ignoring you a little while ago. You see, you didn't come over to the big rock like you always do to meet me, and then I saw you and Cynthia go over to the monkey bars, and you were whispering and laughing. Why? Were you laughing at me?

CARLINE: Deb, you're my best friend. It's just that Cynthia asked me if I'd show her how to cross the monkey bars just once. Since she's new, I want to be nice to her. When we whispered it was about you.

DEB: It was?

CARLINE: Yeah, we were planning to sneak up on you and surprise you and then ask you to join us on the monkey bars. I'd told Cynthia that you were just the nicest girl in the whole school and she wants to get to know you better.

DEB: You told her that?

CARLINE: Sure I did. After all, you are my best friend.

DEB: Thanks, Carline. You're my best friend too.

CARLINE: I'm glad you came to talk to me about this, Deb. I don't like it when we have a conflict. What made you decide to talk to me anyhow?

DEB: Oh, I just got a little help from another friend. Want to meet me at the big rock tomorrow and bring Cynthia?

CARLINE: Sure thing!

Follow-up Questions for Puppet Show Two
DEB GETS THE FACTS

1. What big mistake did Deb make with Carline?

2. How can not getting the facts first make a conflict worse?

3. How can you get the facts first?

4. Since CM cannot be everywhere, how can you handle a conflict when you need to get the facts first?

Puppet Show Three
CARLINE COOLS DOWN

Summary: CM helps Carline think of ways to manage her madness and avoid fouls.

Deb and Carline are on stage.

DEB: Carline, I want to play outside. It's boring in here.

CARLINE: It's too hot to go outside. Besides, yesterday we played outside and played what you wanted. Today I want to play inside.

DEB: You're no fun! I'm going home.

Deb leaves.

CARLINE: Sometimes I get so mad at that Deb. She thinks we always have to do things her way and when she doesn't get her way, she pouts or walks away. I feel so mad right now that I think I might just explode. But I can't explode. I've got to get a grip on myself. Oh, I just don't know what to do.

CM flies in.

CM: I was just flying overhead when I thought I felt someone getting very mad. Would that be you?

CARLINE: Oh, CM, am I glad to see you! I am very mad right now. I feel like there's about nine million steam engines inside my head!

CM: Being mad is okay. You just have to be sure you make good choices about what to do with your madness.

CARLINE: What do you mean?

CM: Well, remember three rules. First, it's not okay to hurt yourself.

CARLINE: Oh, I don't think I'd ever do anything to hurt myself. I'm too special.

CM: Sometimes people hurt themselves and they don't even know it. Like if you hold your angry feelings in and don't do anything to get them out, that's hurting yourself.

CARLINE: It is?

CM: Sure. Whenever we hold feelings inside we may become sick or feel really bad.

CARLINE: Okay, that's one rule. I may not hurt myself. What are the others?

CM: Rule two is you may not hurt property.

CARLINE: Property?

CM: Things are property. Some people think it's okay to slam a door or hit a wall when they are mad. But these ways are not okay ways to get anger out because they could hurt property.

CARLINE: It's not okay to hurt property. What's the third rule?

CM: It's not okay to hurt someone else. This means either their feelings or their body.

CARLINE: Deb hurt my feelings when she said that I was no fun when we were playing.

CM: Deb made a foul.

CARLINE: A foul? You mean like in a soccer game when someone does something against the rules?

CM: Kind of. A foul is something that is said or done that hurts another person's feelings. Fouls make a conflict worse.

CARLINE: I feel like I want to foul Deb back since she did it to me.

CM: You're angry at Deb. But even though she fouled you it's not okay to foul her back. Getting even is a foul. You need to manage your madness and be your own referee.

CARLINE: What do you mean, be my own referee?

CM: Usually in a game, a referee will blow a whistle and stop the game when someone fouls. But when you're having a conflict with someone there is no one to stop the conflict or the fouls by blowing a whistle. You're only in charge of your own behavior, so when you feel yourself getting ready to foul, stop yourself. Take charge of what you say and do—be your own referee.

CARLINE: I get it. But how can I get my madness out?

CM: There are lots of ways. You could count to ten slowly to calm down. Or you could do something to get the anger out like jump rope, dance, or draw a picture. Or you could talk to someone who is not involved in the conflict about your angry feelings.

CARLINE: Well, I've been talking to you, CM, and you know what? I do feel a little calmer. I think I'll try a few more things to get my anger out and then go see if I can work this conflict out with Deb.

CM: Good idea, Carline. Remember you're in charge of your feelings and what you do. I've got to go now and be sure our school is handling their conflicts in a peaceful way. Good–bye, Carline.

CARLINE: Good–bye, CM, and thanks a lot.

CM flies away.

CARLINE: That's one superhero! Now I think I'll do a few more things to get my madness in control. Let's see 1, 2, 3, 4, 5, 6, 7, 8, 9, 10. I feel a little better, but I'm not ready to talk to Deb yet. I think I'll go outside now and ride my bike. Maybe then, I'll feel better. Be sure you tune in next time to see how Deb and I work out our conflict.

CARLINE COOLS DOWN

1. What are the three rules about handling anger?

2. What are fouls?

3. What do fouls do to conflicts?

4. What are some okay ways to manage your madness?

5. Describe a time that someone fouled you when you were having a conflict. How did you feel?

Puppet Show Four
CARLINE COMMUNICATES

Summary: *CM helps Carline learn how to talk to someone when a conflict occurs.*

Carline comes on stage.

CARLINE: Hi, you might remember that the last time I talked to you I was pretty mad at my friend Deb. She got upset because I didn't want to play the same thing she did. She said that I was no fun and she left to go home. CM came and helped me. He told me that I was in charge of my feelings and the things I did. He reminded me that I need to get my madness under control before I do anything else. Well, I talked to CM and that helped. Then I counted to ten and then I rode my bike. Now I'm feeling much better. I need to talk to Deb but I don't know what to say to her. I'm afraid that I might foul her if I say anything. I don't want to hurt Deb's feelings. I just wish I knew how to talk to Deb about our conflict.

CM flies in.

CARLINE: Wow! Am I glad to see you, CM!

CM: Well, I was just flying over on my way to the mall and I thought I sensed that someone needed help with a conflict.

CARLINE: Yes, CM. I need to talk to my friend Deb about our conflict now that I've got my madness under control, but I don't know what to say.

CM: What do you want Deb to know?

CARLINE: Well, I want her to know that my feelings are hurt. And I want her to know why my feelings are hurt. And I want her not to hurt my feelings anymore.

CM: Sounds to me like you could send Deb an "I" message.

CARLINE: A what?

CM: An "I" message. It's a way of telling someone how we feel about something they are doing.

CARLINE: Why do you call it an "I" message?

CM: Because we begin the message with the words "I feel." It's a way to talk about feelings. Here's how it works. First you say the person's name. Try that.

CARLINE: Deb.

CM: Now tell her how you feel.

CARLINE: I feel hurt.

CM: Now tell her why you feel hurt.

CARLINE: Because you leave when you don't get your way.

CM: Now tell her what you want and begin with the word "please."

CARLINE: Please play with me in a nice way.

CM: Now, say the whole thing together.

CARLINE: Deb, I feel hurt when you leave because you don't get your way. Please play with me in a nice way.

CM: Great job. That's part of caring communication. It's talking to someone in a kind way without fouling. The other part has to do with listening.

CARLINE: What about listening?

CM: It's also important to listen in a caring way. When the other person talks, look at them; be sure your body language says that you're listening. After they are done, say something back that shows you're listening.

CARLINE: Do you think it might work for me to send an "I" message to Deb and then listen in a caring way to what she has to say?

CM: It's worth a try. I'm off now to the mall. Good luck, Carline.

CARLINE: Thanks, CM. I think I'll go see Deb now.

Carline leaves. After a pause Deb comes on stage and joins.

CARLINE: Deb, I'd like to talk to you if it's okay.

DEB: Sure.

CARLINE: Deb, I feel hurt when you leave because you don't get your way. Please play with me in a nice way.

DEB: Gee, Carline. I didn't know it upset you so much for me to leave. I thought you wanted me to go when you didn't want to play what I wanted to play.

CARLINE: You thought that just because I wanted to play something different from you that I didn't want to play with you at all?

DEB: I sure did. Did you want to play?

CARLINE: Yes, I did. We might not always agree on what to play, but maybe we can work it out.

DEB: Do you think we could?

CARLINE: I think we can work just about anything out if we care about each other. Maybe CM could help.

VOICE OVER: Be sure to tune in next time when CM helps Deb and Carline work out their conflict.

118

Follow-up Questions for Puppet Show Four
CARLINE COMMUNICATES

1. What are the two parts of communicating?

2. What is an "I" message? What are the four steps to sending an "I" message?

3. What are things that you should do to show someone that you are listening when they are speaking?

4. When can an "I" message be used?

Puppet Show Five
TOOL TIME FOR CARLINE AND DEB

Summary: *Carline and Deb sort through the Timely Tools in order to solve their conflict.*

CM is on stage alone.

CM: In our last show Deb and Carline were having a conflict. Deb got mad and left when Carline didn't do what she wanted. Carline sent Deb an "I" message and Deb and Carline agreed that they would try to work out their conflict. The conflict is that Deb and Carline don't want to do the same thing when they play. Let's join Deb and Carline now and see if I can help them work out their conflict.

CM flies away and Deb and Carline come on stage. CM then flies in to join them.

CARLINE: So, what do we do, Deb, since we can't agree on what we want to do when we are playing together?

DEB: Here's CM. Maybe he can help.

CM: Maybe I can, Deb and Carline. Let me think. There are many ways to work out conflicts. We can call all of those ways tools. Can you think of some of the Timely Tools that you learned about in your class?

CARLINE: I remember a Timely Tool is to postpone if you're too angry to talk about it. But I think that both Deb and I are calm enough to talk about our conflict.

DEB: I think we are too. Ignoring and avoiding are Timely Tools. Could we use them for this conflict?

CM: You're right, Deb. Avoiding and ignoring are Timely Tools, but remember that the tool has to be the right one to get the conflict worked out. Would ignoring or avoiding work in this situation?

DEB: I don't think those are the right tools either. Let me think. Another tool is to apologize. I think that maybe I need to apologize to Carline for leaving when I didn't get my way. I'm sorry I left, Carline.

CARLINE: That's okay, Deb. I just want us to be able to get along when we play. I remembered another tool. It's called compromising.

DEB: What does that mean, Carline?

CARLINE: Compromising is when both people give in a little and come up with a new way to solve the conflict. So instead of me getting my way or you getting your way, we could think of a new idea that we both like.

120

DEB: Yeah, but since I want to play outside and you want to play inside I don't think there's anything in between. Either we play outside or we play inside.

CM: Keep thinking, girls. You'll come up with something.

CARLINE: I remember that another tool is to share. But there's nothing to share here.

DEB: I've got it! I know the tool we could use.

CARLINE: What?

DEB: We could take turns. We could play outside for a little while and then play inside for a little while.

CARLINE: I like that idea! And the tool fits the conflict. Taking turns will work for this conflict. Great idea, Deb.

DEB: Thanks, Carline. Now, let's go play outside first.

CARLINE: Wait a minute. Why do we do what you want first? Why can't we play inside like I want first?

CM: I hear another conflict starting.

CARLINE: Me too. Now that we've decided to take turns, we've got to decide who gets to do their idea first.

DEB: I guess it's back to thinking about the Timely Tools box again.

CARLINE: Another tool was humor but I don't think there's anything to laugh at in this. Except it is kind of funny that once we got through one conflict, it made another!

DEB: That is pretty funny!

All three puppets laugh.

CM: Remember, it's okay to laugh at conflicts but not at people.

CARLINE: Let's keep thinking about how to decide who gets to do their idea first.

DEB: Well another tool is to negotiate. That means to go through all the steps to dealing with problems. But we've really only got two choices here—outside first or inside first.

CARLINE: Hey, I've got it. Chance!

DEB: Huh?

CARLINE: Chance. It's where we let luck decide. CM could choose a number between one and ten. Then we both choose a number and the one closest to the number CM chose gets to do their idea first.

DEB: I like that. Okay, CM, would you pick a number and keep it a secret?

CM: Sure. Okay, I've got it.

DEB: I think it's eight.

CARLINE: I say four.

CM GUY: The number is three. Carline gets to do her idea first.

DEB: That's fair. CM, you sure helped us.

CM: No, Deb. You and Carline helped each other. You talked this conflict out until you came up with a peaceful solution. Even when it got tough, you kept trying to work toward a solution. I think you're both pretty smart.

CARLINE: Thanks, CM. Now, Deb, are you ready to play?

DEB: Sure, Carline. Thanks, CM. See you around.

All puppets exit.

Follow-up Questions for Puppet Show Five
TOOL TIME FOR CARLINE AND DEB

1. How did Deb and Carline cope with their problem?

2. What would have happened if Deb and Carline had fouled each other?

3. What may have happened if one of the girls did not want to work the conflict out?

4. How many Timely Tools can you name?

Recommended Children's Literature with a Conflict Theme

The following is a list of children's literature that can be used to reinforce the four conflict management skills. As you read these stories to children, discuss how they relate to the skills learned in *Coping With Conflict*

Airmail to the Moon by Tom Birdseye
   Ora Mae Cotton learns the importance of being sure of what she says before accusing others. (FACTS FIRST)

Andrew's Angry Words by Dorothea Lachner
   Andrew accidentally lets out some angry words and gets to see firsthand how his angry words and feelings spread quickly. (MADNESS MANAGEMENT)

The Blind Men and the Elephant
   Six blind men give their narrow definition of what an elephant is, but none see the whole picture. (FACTS FIRST)

Chicken Little
   This is a classic tale in which Chicken Little jumps to conclusions after being hit on the head by an apple. (FACTS FIRST)

The Chinese Mirror by Mirra Ginsburg and Margot Zemach
   A traditional Korean tale in which a mirror brought from China causes confusion within a family as each member looks in it and sees a different stranger. (FACTS FIRST)

Green Eggs and Ham by Dr. Seuss
   Sam I Am will not leave his friend alone until he tries the green eggs and ham. (TIMELY TOOLS)

The Hating Book by Charlotte Zolotow
   A misunderstanding that gets out of hand leads friends to a conflict. (FACTS FIRST)

Herbie's Troubles by Carol Chapman
   Herbie tries many ways to handle Jimmy John, the school bully, and ultimately finds the way to do it. (TIMELY TOOLS)

The Hurt by Teddi Doleski
   A conflict between Justin and his friend Gabriel leaves Justin feeling awful and struggling with how to handle his feelings. (MADNESS MANAGEMENT and CARING COMMUNICATION)

I Never Win by Judy Delton
   Charlie becomes increasingly frustrated as he watches everyone else win prizes, but Charlie channels his frustration in a positive direction that proves to have great rewards for him. (MADNESS MANAGEMENT)

I Can't Wait by Elizabeth Crary
   Luke has trouble waiting his turn and students have the opportunity to help Luke problem solve. In this book they make choices about the outcome. (TIMELY TOOLS)

I Want It by Elizabeth Crary
   Children get to help Megan and Amy solve their differences of opinions in this problem solving book. (TIMELY TOOLS)

124

I'm Furious by Elizabeth Crary

Matt becomes angry at his little brother Andy. Students are able to help Matt make choices about his angry feelings in this interactive problem solving book. (MADNESS MANAGEMENT and CARING COMMUNICATION)

The Knight and the Dragon by Tomie dePaola

An inexperienced knight and an inexperienced dragon discover that fighting is not the way to solve differences and learn to work together. (TIMELY TOOLS)

Painting the Fire by Liz Farrington and Johathan Sherwood

With the help of Mrs. Murgatroyd's magical paints, Ryan learns to deal with his anger and to confront the class bully. (MADNESS MANAGEMENT)

The Quarreling Book by Charlotte Zolotow

A family does not deal with their angry feelings and these feelings affect everyone the family encounters during their day. (MADNESS MANAGEMENT)

Six Crows by Leo Lionni

A farmer and six crows are at odds with each other over a field of wheat until a wise old owl helps them find a solution. (TIMELY TOOLS)

The Teacher from the Black Lagoon by Mike Thaler

A boy is frightened when he learns his teacher is Mrs. Green because of the untrue rumors he has heard about her. (FACTS FIRST)

The True Story of the Three Little Pigs by Jon Scieszka

The big bad wolf tells his version of what happened when he met the three little pigs. (FACTS FIRST)

The Three Little Wolves and the Big Bad Pig by Eugene Trivizas and Helen Oxenbury

Three wolves who have just begun life on their own learn ways to deal with an aggressive pig. (TIMELY TOOLS)

Three Wishes by Lucille Clifton

Lena finds a lucky penny and makes a wish that seems to cost her a friendship, but she is able to undo the harm she has done with her third wish. (MADNESS MANAGEMENT)

The Very Angry Day That Amy Didn't Have by Lawrence Shapiro

Amy and Margaret have similar things happen to them in their day but handle things very differently. (MADNESS MANAGEMENT)

Additional Resources

Books:

Creating the Peaceable School (A Comprehensive Program for Teaching Conflict Resolution) by Richard Bodine, Donna Crawford and Fred Scrumpf. (Grades 4-9)
> Research Press
> 2612 North Mattis Avenue
> Champaign, Illinois 61821

Creative Conflict Resolution: More Than 200 Activities for Keeping Peace in the Classroom K-6 by William Kreidler.
> Scott Foresman and Company
> 1900 East Lake Avenue
> Glenview, Illinois 60025

Conflict Resolution: An Elementary School Curriculum by Gail Sadalla, Meg Holmberg, and Jim Halligan.
> The Community Board Program
> 1540 Market Street, #490
> San Francisco, California 94102
> 415-552-1250

Learning the Skills of Peacemaking (A K-6 Activity Guide on Resolving Conflict, Communicating, Cooperating) by Naomi Drew.
> Jalmar Press
> 2675 Skypark Drive, Suite 204
> Torrance, California 90505
> 310-784-0016
> 800-662-9662

Peacemaking Skills for Little Kids - Guide and Student Activity Book by Fran Schmidt, Alice Friedman and Elyse Brunt.
Creative Conflict Solving for Kids (Grades 3-4) by Fran Schmidt and Alice Friedman.
Creative Conflict Solving for Kids (Grades 4-9) by Fran Schmidt and Alice Friedman.
Fighting Fair for Families by Fran Schmidt and Alice Friedman.
> Peace Education Foundation
> 1900 Biscayne Boulevard
> Miami, Florida 33132
> 800-749-8838

Teaching Conflict Resolution Through Children's Literature by William J. Kreidler.
> Scholastic Professional Books
> P.O. Box 7502
> Jefferson City, Missouri 65102
> 800-325-6149

Teaching Students to Be Peacemakers by David Johnson and Roger Johnson.
> Interaction Book Company
> Edina, Minnesota

Videos:

We Can Work It Out: Conflict Resolution (Grades 1-3)
Student Workshop: Solving Conflicts (Grades 2-5)
    Sunburst Communications, Inc.
    39 Washington Avenue
    Pleasantville, New York 10570
    800-431-1934

Donnie Dinosaur in Let's Work It Out (K-1)
    Syndister, Inc.
    125 Mallard Street, Suite A
    St. Rose, Louisiana 70086-9471
    504-468-1100